Sandra Lee
semi-homemade®

desserts

Meredith® Books Des Moines, Iowa

Library of Congress Control Number 2005921342 ISBN: 0-696-22684-7 Published by Meredith® Books. Des Moines, Iowa

dedication

To my fellow Semi-Homemakers,
may God bless you with every decadent dream!

To the sweetest things I've ever known, my nieces and nephews:
Scott, Danielle, Brandon, Austen, Stephanie, Tanner, Brycer, Blakey, and Katie.

To my brothers and sisters, who are thoughtful, loving, supportive, and brilliant:
Cynthia Christi-Lee, Kimber Lee, Richard Christiansen, and John Paul Christiansen.

To my Grandma Lorraine and my Aunt Betty, for all
the sundresses, sundaes, and celebrations.

To the apples of my eye, Aspen and Sunny.

All My Love—Always
S.L.

special thanks

To the Production Team
Ed, George, Hilary, Wes, Jeff, Angie, Denise, Cindy,
Andy, Lane, Lisa, Maryann, Pamela, Jules, Laurent, and Robin.

To the Publishing Team
Jan, Mick, Lisa, Amy, Matt, Erin, Jessica,
Jim, Jeff, Doug, Bob, Jack, and the entire Meredith Family.

To my team of "Great Girlfriends"
Mary, Colleen, Carol, Jane, Julie, Carole, Vinny, Farideh, Cari, Fran,
Hope, Cassandra, Karen, Judy, Tina, Ghada, Alexandra, Arianna, and Isabella.

I'm so incredibly lucky to have you all.

Table of Contents

Chapter 1
From the Package
12

Chapter 2
Chocolatier
30

Chapter 3
American Classics
50

Chapter 4
Celebrity Sweets
66

Chapter 5
Light & Healthy Treats
88

Introduction from Mary Hart

The first thing I thought when I saw my friend Sandra Lee's cookbook was, "This food is absolutely gorgeous." The second thing I thought was, "These recipes are actually doable, even for someone with my crazy schedule!" Here, at last, was food we could all make and enjoy; recipes that make us want to rush right into the kitchen and start cooking, recipes that look as spectacular as they taste.

When Sandra told me her second cookbook was going to be a dessert book, I was thrilled. Sandra loves good food, but she's absolutely passionate about desserts. And I may be a fitness fanatic, but I can seldom pass up a chance to indulge my sweet tooth.

Semi-Homemade® Desserts is more than a collection of recipes; it's a way of life. Sandra loves sharing good food; she loves opening her home to others, making it a beautiful and inviting gathering place for family and friends. But, like so many of us, Sandra's life is busy and full, with much to do and little time to do it in. Her book is an endless stream of ideas, an abundance of simple, yet creative, recipes that are a breeze to make and a treat to serve. Sandra teaches us to have fun with dessert, to try something new, to pair the familiar with the unexpected. She shows us that it's not the grand gestures that impress, but the little touches—a sprinkle of sugared rose petals, a drizzle of warm honey, the cool elegance of fresh mint with lime.

And she does it all with such style. Sandra's desserts are as effervescent and fun to be around as she is. Every dessert is a centerpiece—beautifully prepared, imaginatively garnished and served on a simple white plate, with Sandra's signature touch of playfulness that says, "It is dessert, after all." Whether serving chocolate-covered cherries atop a shot of spiked syrup or tying a big white ribbon around The Perfect Package cake, Sandra knows that a dash of style is as important as a dollop of substance. Whatever the occasion—a bake sale at school, a romantic rendezvous, or a party with friends—you can flip open a Sandra Lee cookbook and know that anything you make will look as sensational as it tastes.

Dessert can be many things—a simple pleasure, a fun extravagance, a delicious way to treat yourself. But most of all, a dessert should be worth every bite. And, for that, Sandra Lee takes the cake.

Here's wishing you sweet success,

Mary Hart

Mary Hart

Letter from Sandra

We all want to have our cake and eat it, too. Now, with Semi-Homemade®, you can have your cake, your cookies, your candies, your cobblers, even your kisses, and eat them, too!

In today's hectic world, with the constant crunch of jobs, families, and errands, it's all too easy to get caught up in the craziness and forget to savor the sweeter side of life. What better way to take a little time for ourselves than with a deliciously decadent dessert that lifts our spirits and makes our taste buds sing?

I've always had a sweet spot for dessert. Growing up, I spent many happy hours watching my grandma bake, helping her sift flour, measure sugars and spices, roll out dough, and decorate each dessert to make it special. To her, and now to me, dessert is love—the delicious byproduct of caring hands and a happy heart. I enjoyed baking with my grandma so much I'd take the money I earned from berry picking or selling handmade crafts and buy the Wilton® books on cake decorating, adding to my collection whenever I could.

As the years went by and time became more precious, I'd search for shortcuts. How could I make each recipe more quickly, saving valuable time while preserving the even more valuable taste? The answer was to mix scratch ingredients with ready-made products from the grocery store, experimenting with the blend until I'd get it just right. I can now proudly say I get the same quality and flavor baking Semi-Homemade® as when I baked from scratch. Of course, the main ingredient in every recipe is still the same—love.

I personally love every single dessert in this book. Each one is unabashedly rich and unapologetically indulgent—a marvelous medley of flavors and textures that lingers lovingly in your mouth. I never feel one bit of guilt. Dessert, like life, is short and sweet. I treasure every melt-in-your-mouth moment and hope you will, too.

This book is full of fast and fabulous treats created with a Semi-Homemaker's busy life in mind. It's created for you and dedicated to you. You'll find desserts for special days … and desserts that make any day special. You'll find desserts to give your family … and desserts to give as gifts. Desserts that satisfy your sweet tooth … and desserts that satisfy your soul.

Dessert is one of life's simple pleasures—especially when made with ease, the Semi-Homemade® way. We all need to take time to smell the roses, particularly when they're buttercream.

With a Big Chocolate Kiss,

Sandra Lee

Shaving

To shave chocolate into elegant curls, drag a sharp vegetable peeler down the side of a block of chocolate (or a chocolate bar), using one fluid motion. The chocolate should be at room temperature.

Trimming

If your oven isn't level or the temperature properly calibrated, cakes may come out uneven. Using a serrated knife, level your cakes by trimming any high spots or rough edges.

Layering

To divide a cake into layers, use a ruler to insert a row of toothpicks evenly around the cooled cake. Using the toothpicks as a guide, gently "saw" the cake horizontally with a sharp serrated knife

Cutting

For perfect slices, dip a chopping knife into hot water and dry it with a towel before every cut. A hot knife cuts more smoothly, and continual cleaning prevents bits of cake from clinging to the slices.

From the Package

HELPFUL HINTS, TIPS, AND TRICKS

CHECKING OVEN: Always preheat the oven 15 minutes before putting cakes in to bake. Buy a spring-action oven thermometer that clips onto your oven rack. An oven that is too hot or too cold can ruin baked goods. Put the rack in the middle of the oven and the cakes in the center of the rack.

BUTTER: Unless specified, use unsalted butter wherever butter is called for.

OILING AND FLOURING PANS: Use real butter when oiling and preparing a cake pan. Not only does the butter impart flavor, but it also makes a nice crust on the outside of the cake. Instead of using flour to flour your cake pans when baking chocolate cakes, use a couple of tablespoons of the dry chocolate cake mix or cocoa powder. The finished cake won't have white streaks from the flour.

TESTING CAKES FOR DONENESS: Insert a toothpick into the center of the cake. If it comes out clean the cake is done. For thicker cake layers a bamboo skewer works well.

COOLING CAKES: Let cakes cool out of the oven for at least 10 to 15 minutes in the cake pan on a rack. Then, when cakes have cooled somewhat, remove them from the pans and transfer to cooling racks until completely cool.

NOTE: Please read each and every chapter opener as there are numerous helpful hints, tips, and tricks to know for fast, fabulous results when making a delicious Semi-Homemade® dessert.

The Recipes

Vanilla Cupcake Bouquet

makes 48 mini cupcakes and 1 cake
prep time 15 minutes **baking time** 45 minutes
cooling time 40 minutes **frosting time** 15 minutes

Anybody can say it with flowers—be unique and say it with cupcakes. A dainty swirl of golden cake blossoms with creamy vanilla centers, this edible bouquet makes a charming centerpiece for an afternoon tea or bridal shower or a gracious gift for anyone with a sweet tooth. To make individual desserts, place three or four cupcake blossoms in a small terra-cotta pot and set one at each place setting. Tint the frosting with food coloring to make a multicolored bouquet or to match your decor.

1   box (18.25-ounce) yellow cake mix, *Duncan Hines Moist Deluxe*®
1¹⁄₃ cups water
¹⁄₂ cup vegetable oil
3   eggs
2   containers (16 ounces each) vanilla frosting, *Betty Crocker Whipped*®
¹⁄₂ cup powdered sugar
48 store-bought mini cupcakes or mini muffins, paper liners removed

Special Equipment
  Pastry bag
  Large star tip

1. Preheat oven to 350 degrees F. Butter and flour 8-inch diameter stainless-steel bowl.

2. Combine cake mix, water, oil, and eggs in large bowl. Beat for 2 minutes or until well blended. Transfer batter to prepared buttered bowl. Bake for 45 minutes or until toothpick inserted into center of cake comes out clean.

3. Cool cake in bowl on cooling rack for 15 minutes. Invert cake onto cooling rack; remove bowl. Cool cake completely. Spread 1 can of frosting over rounded side of cake.

4. Mix remaining can of frosting with powdered sugar in large bowl. Frost or pipe a rosette on top of each cupcake. Place toothpick into bottom of each cupcake; press toothpick into cake dome, forming bouquet. Place cake on cake stand.

Pecan Caramel Cheesecake

servings 12 to 16 **prep time** 10 minutes
chilling time 5 hours

Pecan pie or cheesecake? Try a bite of both with this no-bake New York-style cheesecake smothered in caramelized pecans. The inspired combination of creamy cheesecake, gooey caramel, and crunchy pecans is a two-in-one treat, perfect for parties, special dinners, or starting a new Thanksgiving tradition. Be generous with the caramel—and don't be afraid to let it drip down the sides. It just looks more homemade.

2	boxes (11.1 ounces each) real cheesecake dessert mix, *Jell-O No Bake*®
3/4	cup butter, melted
1/4	cup granulated sugar
2	tablespoons water
2 1/2	cups cold whole milk
1	cup butterscotch caramel sauce, *Mrs. Richardson's*®
1	cup chopped pecans, toasted
1/2	cup packed golden brown sugar

1. Line bottom of 9-inch springform pan with parchment paper.

2. Mix the 2 packages of crust (from the cheesecake dessert mix), the melted butter, sugar, and water in large bowl until well blended. Reserve 1 cup of crumb mixture for topping. Press remaining crumb mixture onto bottom of prepared pan (not up sides).

3. Combine the 2 packages of cheesecake filling and the cold milk in another large bowl. Beat for 3 minutes or until smooth and thick.

4. Fold 1/2 cup of caramel sauce into cheesecake mixture. Pour mixture into crust-lined springform pan. Mix reserved crumb mixture with 1/4 cup of caramel sauce, pecans, and brown sugar. Sprinkle mixture on top of cheesecake.

5. Refrigerate cake at least 5 hours or until set. Run warm knife around pan sides to loosen cake; remove pan sides. Transfer cake to serving platter and drizzle with remaining 1/4 cup of caramel sauce. Serve cold.

Wonton
Napoleons

servings 4 **prep time** 15 minutes
assembly time 10 minutes

Vegetable oil for frying
16 **wonton wrappers (available in the refrigerated Asian foods section)**
1½ **teaspoons ground cinnamon, *McCormick*®**
2 **cups frozen whipped topping, thawed, *Cool Whip*®**
16 **large strawberries, sliced**
1 **pint fresh raspberries**
4 **fresh mint sprigs (optional)**

1. Pour enough oil into small saucepan to come ¼ inch up sides of pan. Heat oil over medium-low heat.

2. Using tongs and working with 1 wonton wrapper at a time, submerge wontons in hot oil, frying until golden brown, about 15 seconds for first side and 10 seconds for second side. Transfer fried wontons to paper towels to drain (wontons will continue to color slightly as they cool). Sprinkle warm fried wontons with cinnamon. Cool completely.

3. To assemble each Napoleon, place 4 fried wontons on work surface. Spread 1 tablespoon of whipped topping over each. Arrange 1 sliced strawberry and 2 to 3 raspberries over the top of each.

4. Spoon 1 tablespoon of whipped topping over berries on each wonton. Top with another fried wonton. Repeat layering two more times. Spoon dollops of remaining whipped topping on top of each stack. Garnish Napoleons with remaining strawberries and raspberries, and mint sprigs (optional). Serve immediately.

Triple Lemon Pound Cake

servings 8 to 10 **prep time** 6 minutes
baking time 45 minutes **cooling time** 30 minutes
frosting time 15 minutes

Cake

1   **box (18.25-ounce) lemon supreme cake mix, *Duncan Hines Moist Deluxe*®**
1   **box (3.9-ounce) lemon instant pudding and pie filling mix, *Jell-O*®**
1   **cup water**
4   **eggs**
$^1/_3$ **cup vegetable oil**
     Zest of one lemon
6   **tablespoons purchased lemon curd, stirred to loosen, *Dickinson's*®**

Lemon Glaze

6   **tablespoons purchased lemon curd, stirred to loosen, *Dickinson's*®**
$^1/_4$ **cup water**
2   **tablespoons fresh lemon juice**
3   **cups powdered sugar**

Cake

1. Preheat oven to 350 degrees F. Butter and flour 12-cup Bundt pan or 13×9-inch metal baking pan.

2. Combine cake mix, pudding mix, water, eggs, oil, and lemon zest in large bowl. Beat for 2 minutes or until well blended. Transfer batter to prepared pan. Drizzle lemon curd on top of batter, keeping curd away from sides of pan.

3. Bake for 45 minutes or until toothpick inserted near center of cake comes out clean. Cool cake in pan on cooling rack for 15 minutes. Invert cake onto cooling rack. Place cooling rack on a cookie sheet. Cool cake completely.

Lemon Glaze

4. Beat lemon curd, water, and lemon juice in large bowl until smooth. Gradually add powdered sugar, beating until mixture is smooth. Drizzle glaze over cake. Transfer cake to serving platter.

Phyllo Pie Bites

servings 12 **prep time** 20 minutes
baking time 20 minutes

8   **plain phyllo pastry sheets (14×8-inch), thawed, *Athens*®**
      Nonstick cooking spray, *PAM*®
¾   **cup cherry preserves, *Smucker's*®**
2   **tablespoons semisweet chocolate morsels, *Nestlé*®**

1. Preheat oven to 375 degrees F. Line cookie sheet with foil.

2. Place 1 phyllo sheet on work surface*. Spray phyllo sheet with cooking spray. Top with second phyllo sheet and spray with cooking spray. Repeat, layering with 2 more phyllo sheets and spraying each, for a total stack of 4 phyllo sheets.

3. Cut stacked phyllo sheets into 6 even squares. Spoon 1 scant tablespoon of cherry preserves into center of each square. Sprinkle ½ teaspoon chocolate morsels over preserves. Enclose filling by gathering phyllo and pinching tops tightly to form purses.

4. Transfer phyllo purses to prepared cookie sheet. Repeat with remaining 4 phyllo sheets, cooking spray, preserves, and chocolate morsels. Bake for 20 minutes or until phyllo is crisp and golden. Cool pastries on cookie sheet.

***Note:** Keep phyllo dough sheets covered until needed, since they dry out quickly when exposed to air.

Sweet Sorbet Spritzer

servings 4
prep time 5 minutes

This colorful cocktail has all the shades of a Caribbean sunset and the sultry indolence of a long summer night. A swirl of sweet mango, the festive fizz of ginger ale, and a splash of smooth sorbet combine in a kick-back cooler as light and refreshing as an island breeze. Grab a few goblets, throw off your shoes, and drink in the allure of the islands. Wherever you happen to be, this drink is nirvana in a glass.

1   cup canned mango nectar, chilled, *Kerns*®
1   pint mango sorbet, *Häagen-Dazs*®
1   pint strawberry sorbet, *Dreyer's*® or *Edy's*®
2   cups ginger ale, chilled, *Canada Dry*®

1. Divide mango nectar among 4 chilled glasses. Scoop sorbets into glasses. Slowly pour ginger ale over sorbets. Serve immediately.

Mango Margaritas

servings 2
prep time 5 minutes

   Granulated sugar
$^1/_2$ **lime, cut into quarters**
$^1/_2$ **cup tequila**
$^2/_3$ **cup mango nectar, *Kerns*®**
3   **tablespoons bottled lime juice, *ReaLime*®**
1   **cup medium ice cubes**

1. Spread thin layer of sugar on a saucer. Run 1 lime wedge around rim of each of 2 margarita or martini glasses. Press rims into sugar on saucer to create narrow sugared edge on each glass.

2. In a cocktail shaker or small pitcher, combine tequila, mango nectar, lime juice, and ice cubes. Shake or stir vigorously for 30 seconds. Strain equal amounts into each glass. Squeeze juice from 1 lime wedge into each drink and drop lime wedge in. Serve immediately.

Note: For a nonalcoholic margarita, omit tequila; reduce ice cubes to $^1/_2$ cup; place mango nectar, lime juice, and ice cubes in blender set on frappe; process until smooth.

Chocolatier

HELPFUL HINTS, TIPS, AND TRICKS

MELTING CHOCOLATE: Stir dark or milk chocolate as it melts to keep it smooth. If the cocoa butter crystals in the chocolate come in contact with any moisture during melting, they may cause the chocolate to seize. For this reason, never cover chocolate when melting; moisture may get trapped inside the bowl or pot and drip back into the chocolate, causing it to become thick and lumpy. The same can happen if the chocolate is melted over rapidly simmering or boiling water, which causes steam. If the chocolate seizes, try stirring in a teaspoon of vegetable or canola oil for every 12 ounces of chocolate. However, this trick may not work and the only remedy may be to start over.

MELTING CHOCOLATE IN THE MICROWAVE: For chocolate morsels, place morsels in a glass bowl and microwave on medium power at 30-second intervals, stirring between intervals. The chocolate is done when it looks shiny and stirs easily into a smooth pool.

MELTING CHOCOLATE OVER A DOUBLE BOILER: You can use a conventional double boiler or a pot with a stainless-steel bowl set on top. Fill bottom pot with a few inches of water and bring to a very gentle simmer. The water should not touch the bottom of the upper pot or bowl or the chocolate might scorch. Stir frequently until the chocolate melts completely and is very smooth.

NOTE: Please read each and every chapter opener as there are numerous helpful hints, tips, and tricks to know for fast, fabulous results when making a delicious Semi-Homemade® dessert.

The Recipes

Chocolate Thumbprint Cookies

makes about 48 cookies
prep time 25 minutes
chilling time 30 minutes

1   container (16-ounce) dark chocolate frosting,
        Betty Crocker Rich & Creamy®
$^1/_2$ stick butter, softened
$2^1/_2$ cups graham cracker crumbs, *Nabisco Honey Maid®*
$^1/_2$ teaspoon pure almond extract, *McCormick®*
1   cup very finely ground almonds
48   (about) large chocolate morsels, unwrapped, *Hershey's Kisses®*

1. Beat chocolate frosting and butter in large bowl until well blended. Mix in graham cracker crumbs and almond extract. Place almonds in pie pan or other shallow bowl.

2. Shape chocolate mixture into 1-inch balls (about 48). Roll each ball in almonds to coat. Place balls on cookie sheet.

3. Using finger, make deep indentation in center of each ball. Fill each indentation with large chocolate morsel. Refrigerate for 30 minutes or until cold.

Frozen English Toffee Cake

servings 12 to 16 **prep time** 15 minutes
baking time 30 minutes **cooling time** 30 minutes
assembly time 15 minutes **freezing time** 3 hours
standing time 5 minutes

Cake
1   box (18.25-ounce) devil's food cake mix, *Duncan Hines Moist Deluxe®*
1⅓ cups water
½   cup vegetable oil
3   eggs

Ice Cream Filling and Frosting
½   gallon chocolate or vanilla ice cream, softened, *Dreyer's®* or *Edy's®*
1   bag (10-ounce) English toffee bits, *SKOR®*
1   container (8-ounce) frozen whipped topping, thawed, *Cool Whip®*

Cake
1. Preheat oven to 350 degrees F. Butter and flour two 8-inch round cake pans.

2. Combine cake mix, water, oil, and eggs in large bowl. Beat for 2 minutes or until well blended. Pour batter into prepared pans. Bake for 30 minutes or until toothpick inserted into centers of cakes comes out clean. Cool cakes in pans on cooling rack for 15 minutes. Remove cakes from pans and cool cakes completely on cooling rack.

Ice Cream Filling
3. Line three 8-inch round cake pans with plastic wrap, allowing 3 inches of plastic to hang over sides. Divide ice cream equally among pans. Using rubber spatula, spread ice cream over bottoms of prepared pans, forming smooth, even layers. Sprinkle ¼ cup of toffee bits over ice cream in each pan. Freeze for 3 hours or until frozen solid.

Assembly and Frosting
4. Cut each cake layer horizontally in half. Working quickly, remove ice cream from pans. Peel off plastic and place 1 ice cream circle on each of 3 cake layers. Stack cake and ice cream layers on top of each other on serving platter. Top with remaining cake layer. Frost cake with whipped topping and sprinkle with remaining toffee bits. Freeze until ready to serve. Let ice cream cake stand at room temperature for 5 minutes before serving.

Viennese Ice Cream Cake

servings 8 to 10 **prep time** 40 minutes
freezing time 6 hours **standing time** 10 minutes

2   packages (5.5 ounces each, 20 sticks total) chocolate caramel cookie bars, *Twix®*
1   quart coffee ice cream, softened, *Häagen-Dazs®*
³/₄ cup butterscotch caramel topping, *Mrs. Richardson's®*
³/₄ cup chopped pecans, toasted
1   quart vanilla ice cream, softened, *Dreyer's®* or *Edy's®*
1   container (8-ounce) frozen whipped topping, thawed, *Cool Whip®*
1   (1.55-ounce) milk chocolate candy bar, shaved, *Hershey's®*

Special Equipment
Pastry bag
#6 star tip

1. Line 9¹/₄×5×2³/₄-inch loaf pan with 2 layers of plastic wrap, allowing 3 inches of plastic to hang over pan sides. Stand cookies along sides of prepared pan, spacing evenly. Using rubber spatula, press one-fourth of coffee ice cream into pan. Drizzle about 1 tablespoon of caramel topping over ice cream. Sprinkle about 1 tablespoon of pecans over caramel. Spread one-fourth of vanilla ice cream over nuts. Drizzle about 1 tablespoon of caramel topping over ice cream; sprinkle about 1 tablespoon of pecans over caramel.

2. Freeze 20 minutes or until firm. Repeat, layering coffee ice cream, caramel, pecans, and vanilla ice cream 3 more times, freezing for 20 minutes between each layering. Fold plastic overhang on top of cake to cover. Freeze for 4 hours or until frozen solid.

3. To unmold, wrap hot damp towels around pan to loosen ice cream cake from pan. Fold back plastic from top of ice cream cake. Invert large plate or serving platter on top of ice cream cake. Holding plate and pan together, invert cake onto plate. Remove pan from cake; peel off plastic wrap. Spoon whipped topping into pastry bag fitted with star tip. Pipe stripes or fluted lines on top of cake.

4. Freeze for 1 hour or until whipped topping is frozen solid. Let cake stand at room temperature 10 minutes before serving. Sprinkle chocolate shavings over cake. Cut cake crosswise into slices; transfer cake slices to plates.

Crispy Orange
Coconut Balls

makes 24 coconut balls
prep time 30 minutes

Crunchy milk chocolate with an undertone of orange and a coating of crisp coconut make these bite-size balls the dessert to serve when you're looking for something a bit different—and a bit more fun. Stack them in individual parfait glasses or in playful coconut shell goblets to liven up your tablescape, or heap them in a serve-yourself basket for a buffet. To hand them out as party favors, slip a handful into a decorative bag or box, tie with a colorful ribbon, and send your guests home with sweet memories of the evening.

1   container (16-ounce) dark chocolate fudge or milk chocolate
        frosting, *Duncan Hines Creamy Home-Style®*
2³⁄₄ cups powdered sugar, sifted
2   teaspoons pure orange extract, *McCormick®*
1¹⁄₂ cups chocolate-flavored sweetened rice cereal, *Kellogg's Cocoa
        Rice Krispies®*
2   cups sweetened flaked coconut, toasted, *Baker's®*

1. Line cookie sheet with waxed paper. Beat frosting and powdered sugar in large bowl until well blended. Beat in orange extract. Stir in rice cereal.

2. Using tablespoon or 1-ounce cookie scoop, shape mixture into balls and place on prepared cookie sheet. Cover and refrigerate for 20 minutes or until slightly firm. Roll balls in coconut to coat. Cover and refrigerate until ready to serve.

Frozen Cookie Cake

servings 12 to 16 **prep time** 10 minutes
baking time 25 minutes **cooling time** 30 minutes
chilling time 1½ hours **freezing time** 3 hours
standing time 5 minutes

Cake
1   **box (18.25-ounce) devil's food cake mix, *Duncan Hines Moist Deluxe*®**
1½ **cups water**
½   **cup vegetable oil**
3   **eggs**

Ganache and Filling
1   **cup heavy cream**
1   **bag (12-ounce) semisweet chocolate morsels, *Nestlé*®**
½   **gallon cookies 'n cream ice cream, softened, *Dreyer's*® or *Edy's*®**

Cake
1. Preheat oven to 350 degrees F. Butter and flour two 10-inch round cake pans. Combine cake mix, water, oil, and eggs in large bowl. Beat for 2 minutes or until well blended. Divide batter between prepared pans. Bake for 25 minutes or until toothpick inserted into centers of cakes comes out clean. Cool cakes in pans on cooling rack for 15 minutes. Remove cakes from pans and cool cakes completely on cooling rack.

Ganache
2. Heat cream in small saucepan over low heat until small bubbles appear around edges. Remove pan from heat. Add chocolate morsels and stir until ganache mixture is smooth. Refrigerate ganache until cool and slightly thickened, stirring occasionally, about 30 minutes. Spread ganache over top and sides of each cake. Refrigerate cakes for 1 hour or until ganache is set.

Filling
3. Line one 9-inch round cake pan with plastic wrap, allowing 3 inches of plastic to hang over pan sides. Using spatula, spread ice cream in prepared pan, forming smooth, even layer. Freeze for 3 hours or until frozen solid.

4. To assemble, place 1 cake layer, ganache side up, on serving platter. Remove ice cream circle from pan; peel off plastic. Place ice cream circle on top of cake. Top with second cake layer, ganache side up. Freeze until ready to serve. Let finished cake stand at room temperature for 5 minutes before serving.

Variation: Use a wooden skewer to write on and decorate ganache on top of cake to make this cake look even more like a chocolate sandwich cookie.

Chocolate Bundt Cake with Ganache

servings 8 to 10 **prep time** 8 minutes
baking time 45 minutes **cooling time** 40 minutes
frosting time 15 minutes

Ganache is a smooth mixture of melted chocolate and cream that hardens to a glossy glaze. Drizzle it over a moist, spongy Bundt cake for a dressy dessert that pairs perfectly with coffee. It's a gorgeous treat for company or an ideal indulgence any time of day—breakfast, brunch, or dinner.

Cake
- 1 box (18.25-ounce) Swiss chocolate cake mix, *Duncan Hines Moist Deluxe®*
- 1 box (3.9-ounce) chocolate instant pudding and pie filling mix, *Jell-O®*
- 1 cup water
- 4 eggs
- 1/3 cup vegetable oil
- 1/2 cup (4 ounces) semisweet chocolate morsels, *Nestlé®*

Ganache
- 1 cup heavy cream
- 1 package (12-ounce) semisweet chocolate morsels, *Nestlé®*
  Additional semisweet chocolate morsels, *Nestlé®* (optional)

Cake
1. Preheat oven to 350 degrees F. Butter and flour 12-cup Bundt pan. Combine cake mix, pudding mix, water, eggs, and oil in large bowl. Beat for 2 minutes or until well blended. Stir in the 1/2 cup chocolate morsels. Transfer batter to prepared Bundt pan. Bake for 45 minutes or until toothpick inserted near center of cake comes out clean. Cool cake in pan on cooling rack for 15 minutes. Invert cake onto cooling rack. Place cooling rack on top of cookie sheet. Cool cake completely.

Ganache
2. Heat cream in small saucepan over low heat until small bubbles appear. Remove from heat. Add the 12 ounces of chocolate morsels to cream and stir until smooth. Cool ganache just until slightly warm. Pour ganache over cooled cake, coating cake completely. Transfer cake to serving platter. Garnish with additional chocolate morsels (optional).

Peanut Butter
Mini Mud Pies

servings 6 **prep time** 10 minutes
freezing time 1 hour

6 tablespoons creamy peanut butter, *Jif®*
6 mini graham cracker crusts, *Keebler Ready Crust®*
3½ cups (from 1 quart) coffee ice cream, *Häagen-Dazs®*
1 bottle (7-ounce) milk chocolate shell topping, *Hershey's®*
1 tablespoon graham cracker crumbs, *Nabisco Honey Maid®*

1. Spread 1 tablespoon peanut butter into bottom of each mini crust. Using ½-cup or 4-ounce ice cream scoop, place ball of ice cream on each crust. Freeze for at least 1 hour or until ice cream and crusts are frozen solid.

2. Remove pies from foil pie tins; place pies on plates. Drizzle chocolate shell topping over ice cream in crusts. Immediately sprinkle ½ teaspoon of crumbs over each pie and serve.

Variation: To make mini chocolate piecrusts, scrape the filling from Oreo® cookies, then finely grind the cookies in a food processor. Set aside 1 tablespoon of cookie crumbs for garnish. Mix the crumbs with just enough melted butter to moisten lightly. Press the crumb mixture over the sides and bottoms of 6 mini pie pans.

Chocolate Box with Easy Chocolate Mousse

Makes 1 box **prep time** 15 minutes
chilling time 20 minutes

1   cup frozen whipped topping, thawed, *Cool Whip®*
2   containers (3.5 ounces each) prepared chocolate-flavored pudding,
        Kraft Handi-Snacks®
3   chocolate bars (4.5 ounces each), milk chocolate or
        bittersweet chocolate, *Cadbury®*
1   container (16-ounce) chocolate frosting, *Pillsbury Creamy Supreme®*
     Fresh raspberries

Special Equipment
    Pastry bag
    Large star tip

1. Place whipped topping and pudding in large bowl. Using rubber spatula, fold just until blended. Refrigerate chocolate mousse until ready to serve.

2. Cut chocolate bars crosswise in half. Attach sides with chocolate frosting to form box (see photo, below). Refrigerate until firm, about 20 minutes.

3. Fill pastry bag with chocolate mousse and pipe into chilled chocolate box. Top with raspberries and serve.

Note: The chocolate mousse is also delicious on its own. Serve it in large wine goblets and garnish with whipped topping and raspberries for an elegant presentation.

White Chocolate Macadamia Nut Bark

makes 1 1/2 pounds
prep time 10 minutes **chilling time** 30 minutes

2   **cups semisweet chocolate morsels, *Nestlé*®**
2   **cups white vanilla milk chips, *Guittard Choc-Au-Lait*®**
2/3 **cup macadamia nuts or almonds, toasted and coarsely chopped**

1. Line 13×9-inch cookie sheet with waxed paper, allowing 2 inches of paper to hang over sides.

2. Melt 1 3/4 cups semisweet chocolate morsels in microwave on medium power for 2 minutes, stirring every 30 seconds, or until smooth. Pour melted semisweet chocolate onto prepared sheet and spread to cover entire surface and form 1 even layer.

3. Melt 1 3/4 cups of white chips in microwave on medium power for 2 minutes, stirring every 30 seconds, or until smooth. Drizzle melted white chips over semisweet chocolate layer. Using toothpick or skewer, swirl melted chocolates together, creating marbled effect. Sprinkle with nuts and remaining 1/4 cup semisweet chocolate morsels and 1/4 cup white chips. Gently press toppings into melted chocolates.

4. Refrigerate for 30 minutes or until chocolate is firm. Remove waxed paper from chocolate. Cut or break chocolate into bite-size pieces.

Almond Haystacks

makes 12 pieces
prep time 10 minutes **chilling time** 30 minutes

1   **bag (12-ounce) semisweet chocolate morsels, *Nestlé*®**
2   **cups slivered almonds, toasted**

1. Line cookie sheet with parchment paper or waxed paper. Melt chocolate in microwave on medium power for 2 minutes, stirring every 30 seconds, or until smooth.

2. Using 1 tablespoon of chocolate for each, spoon 12 chocolate circles onto prepared sheet, spacing evenly. Sprinkle each chocolate circle with 1 tablespoon of almonds. Refrigerate for 10 minutes or until chocolate is firm.

3. Rewarm remaining melted chocolate and drizzle 1 teaspoon into center of each chocolate-nut circle. Top each with 1 teaspoon of almonds. Refrigerate for 10 minutes or until chocolate is firm. Repeat layering one more time, adding as much height to stacks as possible.

American Classics

HELPFUL HINTS, TIPS, AND TRICKS

FROSTING CAKES: Frosting can become difficult to handle if it becomes too warm. If this happens, place the cake and frosting in the refrigerator for 10 minutes to chill.

FREEZING CAKES: After cakes have cooled completely, wrap tightly in plastic wrap, then in aluminum foil. Cakes can be kept frozen for up to three months.

FREEZING FROSTED CAKES: If cakes are frosted, place them in the freezer until frosting is firm, then wrap them the same way as unfrosted cakes.

THAWING FROZEN CAKES: Remove wrapping, then place cake in an airtight container. Allow cake to defrost in the refrigerator overnight, then bring to room temperature before serving.

NOTE: Please read each and every chapter opener as there are numerous helpful hints, tips, and tricks to know for fast, fabulous results when making a delicious Semi-Homemade® dessert.

The Recipes

Port of San Francisco Sundae

servings 4 **prep time** 10 minutes
cooking time 10 minutes

This vintage childhood favorite looks like it's right out of *Willy Wonka and the Chocolate Factory* but with a grown-up twist—a brown sugar-port sauce and elegant white chocolate. Every bite brings a burst of flavors and textures—chunky chocolate, velvety hot fudge, sugary ruby port, and fluffy froths of whipped cream. I serve it in a clear goblet so you can see how wonderfully the colors blend. The recipe makes one cup of Port Sauce—enough for four sundaes. If you really want to do it up, garnish the top with a chocolate-covered cherry (recipe on page 171).

Port Sauce
2 **cups ruby port, *Christian Brothers*®**
1$^1/_2$ **cups packed golden brown sugar**

Sundae
1 **quart vanilla or chocolate chip ice cream, *Häagen-Dazs*®**
$^1/_2$ **cup chocolate hot fudge topping, warm, *Hershey's*®**
$^1/_4$ **cup premier white morsels, *Nestlé*®**

Port Sauce
1. Bring port and sugar to boil in heavy small saucepan over high heat. Reduce heat and simmer for 10 minutes or until mixture is syrupy and equals 1 cup. Cool sauce slightly.

Sundae
2. Scoop ice cream into 4 wineglasses or sundae dishes. Spoon hot fudge topping over ice cream, then spoon $^1/_4$ cup of warm port sauce over each sundae. Sprinkle with white morsels. Serve immediately.

Tip: Port Sauce can be made 1 day ahead. Cover and refrigerate. Rewarm in microwave.

Philadelphia Sour Cream Cherry Cheesecake

servings 8 **prep time** 10 minutes **baking time** 10 minutes **chilling time** 45 minutes

1   box (11.2-ounce) homestyle cheesecake dessert mix, *Jell-O No Bake®*
¾   stick butter, melted
2   tablespoons granulated sugar
1⅓ cups cold whole milk
⅓   cup sour cream
1   container (21-ounce) cherry pie filling or topping, *Comstock More Fruit®*

1. Preheat oven to 350 degrees F. Stir the packet of crust mix (from the cheesecake dessert mix) with melted butter and sugar in large bowl until crumbs are moistened. Press crumb mixture onto bottom of 9-inch springform pan. Bake until crust is set and golden brown around edges, about 10 minutes. Pat down crust. Refrigerate crust for 15 minutes or until cooled completely.

2. Combine cheesecake filling mix, milk, and sour cream in another large bowl. Beat for 2 minutes or until smooth. Pour cheesecake filling mixture over crust. Refrigerate for 30 minutes or until filling is set.

3. To unmold, carefully remove sides from pan and place cheesecake on serving platter. Using sharp knife, cut cake into wedges; transfer to plates. Spoon cherry pie filling over and serve.

Award-Winning New York Blintzes

makes 6 **prep time** 20 minutes

1   cup sour cream
2½ tablespoons granulated sugar
½   cup cream cheese, room temperature, *Philadelphia®*
1½ cups cherry pie filling or topping, *Comstock More Fruit®*
¼   cup semisweet chocolate mini morsels, *Nestlé®*
1   teaspoon lemon zest
6   purchased 7-inch square crepes, *Frieda's®*,
       or 6 purchased 9-inch round crepes, *Melissa's®*
3   tablespoons butter

1. Mix sour cream and sugar in small bowl to blend; set aside. Beat cream cheese in large bowl until fluffy. Stir 1 cup cherry pie filling, chocolate morsels, and lemon zest into cream cheese. Place 1 crepe on work surface; spoon 3 tablespoons of cream cheese mixture into center of crepe. Fold bottom of crepe over filling, then fold opposite side of crepe over. Repeat with remaining crepes and cream cheese mixture.

2. Melt 1 tablespoon of butter on large nonstick griddle over medium-low heat. Place 2 blintzes, seam sides down, in hot butter. Fry for 2 minutes on each side, or until crepes are golden and filling is heated through. Transfer blintzes to serving plates.

3. Repeat with remaining blintzes, adding more butter to griddle as needed. Top with sweetened sour cream and remaining cherry pie filling and serve.

Variation: Fold bottom of crepe over filling. Fold in sides and roll up.

Texas Cinnamon
Pecan Strudel

makes 10 to 12 slices
prep time 10 minutes **baking time** 20 minutes

1 package (18-ounce) frozen unbaked cinnamon rolls, thawed, *Rich's*®
3 tablespoons honey, *Sue Bee*®
½ cup chopped pecans
½ cup chopped walnuts
   Additional honey, *Sue Bee*®
1 teaspoon ground cinnamon, *McCormick*®

1. Preheat oven to 375 degrees F. Line cookie sheet with parchment paper.

2. Gather cinnamon rolls into one ball. Knead dough in bowl until smooth. Roll out dough on lightly floured work surface to 12×7-inch rectangle. Brush dough with 3 tablespoons honey. Sprinkle dough with pecans and walnuts. Gently press nuts into dough. Roll up dough as for jelly roll.

3. Place dough, seam side down, on prepared cookie sheet. Bake for 20 minutes, or until golden brown. Cut strudel crosswise into diagonal slices. Drizzle with additional honey and sprinkle with cinnamon. Serve warm.

Los Angeles Lemon Almond Cake

servings 8 to 10 **prep time** 10 minutes
baking time 30 minutes **cooling time** 40 minutes
frosting time 15 minutes

A masterpiece of contrasting flavors and textures—toasted coconut, crunchy almonds, and tart lemon—this lavish confection is the cake to make when ordinary just won't do. The coconut gives the cake a lacy, old-fashioned look, so I serve it on vintage china or chintzware to play up the mood. Matching the dessert to the plates is one of my favorite tricks.

1   box (18.25-ounce) lemon cake mix, *Betty Crocker SuperMoist®*
1 1/4 cups water
1/3 cup vegetable oil
3   eggs
1/2 cup ground almonds
2 1/2 cups sweetened flaked coconut, very lightly toasted, *Baker's®*
1   can (16-ounce) lemon frosting, *Betty Crocker Rich & Creamy®*
3   ounces sliced almonds, toasted

1. Preheat oven to 350 degrees F. Butter and flour two 8- or 9-inch round cake pans.

2. Combine cake mix, water, oil, and eggs in large bowl. Beat for 2 minutes or until well blended. Stir in ground almonds and 1/2 cup coconut. Divide batter between prepared pans.

3. Bake for 30 minutes or until toothpick inserted into centers of cakes comes out clean. Cool cakes in pans on cooling rack for 15 minutes. Invert cakes onto cooling rack; remove pans. Cool cakes completely.

4. Place 1 cake layer on serving platter. Spread 1/2 cup frosting over cake layer on platter. Top with second cake layer. Frost top and sides of cake with remaining frosting. Press sliced almonds around cake sides.Sprinkle top with remaining 2 cups coconut.

Note: To toast shredded coconut or almonds, preheat oven to 350 degrees F. Place coconut (or almonds) on baking sheet. Toast for 6 to 8 minutes or until coconut (or almonds) turns light brown.

Colorado Chocolate Peaks

makes 20 cupcakes **prep time** 30 minutes
baking time 12 minutes **cooling time** 15 minutes

Cupcakes

1⅓ cups hot water
2   tablespoons instant coffee crystals, *Maxwell House*®
1   box (18.3-ounce) chocolate fudge cake mix, *Betty Crocker SuperMoist*®
⅓   cup vegetable oil
3   eggs
20   soft caramel candies, unwrapped, *Brach's Milk Maid*®

Filling and Topping

1   container (16-ounce) chocolate frosting, *Betty Crocker Rich & Creamy*®
1   jar (7-ounce) marshmallow creme, chilled, *Kraft Jet-Puffed*®
¼   cup unsweetened cocoa powder, *Hershey's*®
¼   cup sweetened flaked coconut, toasted, *Baker's*®

1. Preheat oven to 350 degrees F. Butter and flour 20 cups in two 12-cup muffin pans. For the cupcakes, stir the 1⅓ cups hot water and coffee crystals in large bowl until crystals dissolve. Let cool. Add cake mix, oil, and eggs to coffee in large bowl. Beat 2 minutes or until well blended.

2. Fill each muffin cup halfway with batter. Place 1 caramel in center of each. Pour remaining batter over caramels. Bake for 12 minutes or until cakes have puffed. Cool cupcakes in pans on racks for 15 minutes. Carefully remove cupcakes from pans.

3. To assemble, cut off tops of cupcakes; reserve tops. Frost cupcake bottoms with chocolate frosting. Spoon 1 tablespoon of chilled marshmallow creme on each frosted bottom. Replace cake tops. Dust with cocoa powder, sprinkle with coconut, and serve.

Seattle Morning Coffee Cake

makes 12 to 16 slices **prep time** 10 minutes
baking time 45 minutes **cooling time** 25 minutes

7   sweet dinner rolls, *King's Hawaiian*®
1   box (1-pound 14-ounce) cinnamon swirl coffee cake mix, *Pillsbury*®
¾   cup water
¼   cup vegetable oil
3   eggs
1   cup whole milk
1   tablespoon granulated sugar

1. Preheat oven to 350 degrees. Butter and flour 10-cup Bundt pan. Slice 1 inch off tops of rolls and tear tops into 1-inch pieces; set aside. Place bottoms of rolls, cut sides up, in prepared pan.

2. Combine coffee cake batter mix, water, oil, and 2 of the eggs in large bowl. Beat until well blended. Pour half of batter over rolls. Sprinkle with cinnamon swirl packet from coffee cake mix. Pour remaining batter over rolls. Whisk the remaining 1 egg, the milk, and sugar in another bowl to blend. Add reserved roll tops to milk mixture; set aside until milk mixture is absorbed. Pour roll top mixture over cake batter in pan. Swirl batters together with a skewer.

3. Bake for 45 minutes or until toothpick inserted near center of cake comes out clean. Cool cake in pan for 25 minutes. Invert cake onto cooling rack; remove pan. Place cake, right side up, on platter. Slice cake and serve.

Celebrity Sweets

MAKING A DIFFERENCE

While creating this chapter, I was amazed to learn that these talented personalities seen on TV, stage, and the "Big Screen" have lives surprisingly similar to yours and mine. They're busy working people with families that depend on them, responsibilities that consume them, and convictions that drive them. They cook and clean, decorate their homes, go to work, and entertain friends. They're simply everyday people with high-profile jobs; thoughtful and caring, they lend their time and support to causes that help their communities and those less fortunate. They, like us, know that one person can make a difference and how much bigger that difference will be if we all chip in.

These two worthy organizations make a difference every day:

- Founded in 1989, Project Angel Food prepares and delivers more than 1,000 free meals daily to men, women, and children disabled by HIV/AIDS and other terminal illnesses, such as diabetes, cancer, and Parkinson's. In Project Angel Food's kitchen, you can find Eric McCormack cooking, Queen Latifah directing, Anthony Edwards serving, and Kristin Davis acting as sous chef. To lend your own helping hands, please visit PAF's website at www.angelfood.org or call 1-800-59-ANGEL.

- In 2000, the National Colorectal Cancer Research Alliance (NCCRA) was co-founded by Katie Couric, Lilly Tartikoff, and the Entertainment Industry Foundation (EIF) to raise awareness and research dollars in the fight against colon cancer. Katie lost her husband, Jay Monahan, to the disease in 1998 when he was 42 years old. The NCCRA supports cutting-edge research conducted by leading scientists that has already produced significant advances. For more information, visit the NCCRA at www.nccra.org or call 1-800-872-3000.

"When you learn … teach. When you get … give."
—From Oprah Winfrey's acceptance speech, 2002 Emmy Awards

The Recipes

The day starts early for Katie Couric. By the time most of us roll out of bed, Katie's already been on the job for hours—and will be there for many more. Two young children and long workdays mean every minute counts in Katie's hectic household. Fortunately, this easy-bake breakfast ring will get anyone's morning off to a fruitful start. The shortcut is refrigerated crescent dough, filled with raspberry jam and drizzled with an elegant almond glaze. Perfect for today—or any day.

Katie Couric's Early Morning Raspberry Crescent Ring

servings 12 **prep time** 20 minutes
baking time 25 minutes **cooling time** 10 minutes

Crescent Ring
2 **containers (8 ounces each) refrigerated crescent roll dough, *Pillsbury*®**
1 **container (7-ounce) pure almond paste, *Odense*®**
¼ **cup seedless red raspberry jam or cherry jam**

Glaze
1 **cup powdered sugar**
1½ **tablespoons water**
¼ **teaspoon pure almond extract, *McCormick*®**
   Sugar-dipped cherries and small pears (optional)

Crescent Ring
1. Preheat oven to 375 degrees F. Line heavy large cookie sheet with parchment paper.

2. Unroll crescent dough; separate along dough perforations into 16 triangles. Overlap 8 dough triangles on prepared baking sheet, positioning longest points in center and forming 10-inch dough disk. Press edges of triangles together to seal. Using rolling pin, roll out almond paste between 2 sheets of waxed paper into 9-inch disk.

3. Remove waxed paper and place almond paste disk on top of dough disk. Spread jam over almond paste. Using remaining 8 dough triangles, arrange second 10-inch dough disk on top of jam. Pinch edges of dough disks to seal. Tuck edges under. Bake for 25 minutes or until golden brown. Remove from oven and cool for 10 minutes.

Glaze
4. Stir powdered sugar, water, and almond extract in medium bowl until smooth. Drizzle half of glaze over warm crescent. Let glaze set for 10 minutes. Drizzle remaining glaze over top. Decorate with sugar-dipped cherries and pears (optional).

Eric McCormack loves food. After all, the **Will & Grace** star lured his wife into marriage with his "Love Salad" recipe—just think what he can do with biscotti! The irresistible pairing of deep, dark chocolate and smoky almond is sure to steal hearts, and it's amazingly easy to make—a must when you have a small child and a hit TV show requiring long days on the set. Who knows? This stylish snack might make a guest appearance in Will Truman's kitchen.

Join Emmy-winner Eric for a night of laughs—and possibly dessert—on NBC's **Will & Grace**.

Eric McCormack's Amazing Chocolate Almond Biscotti

makes 26 biscotti **prep time** 10 minutes
baking time 1 1/2 hours **cooling time** 1 hour

1	box (18.25-ounce) dark chocolate fudge or devil's food cake mix, *Duncan Hines Moist Deluxe®*
1	cup all-purpose flour
1	stick butter, melted
2	eggs
2	teaspoons pure almond extract, *McCormick®*
3/4	cup whole almonds

1. Preheat oven to 350 degrees F. Line 2 heavy large cookie sheets with parchment paper.

2. Combine cake mix, flour, melted butter, eggs, and almond extract in large bowl. Beat for 2 minutes or until dough forms. Knead almonds into dough. Scrape dough onto 1 of the prepared baking sheets and form dough into a log that is 13 inches long and 3 inches wide.

3. Bake for 35 minutes or until toothpick inserted into center of biscotti comes out clean. Cool for 35 minutes. Using serrated knife, cut log crosswise into 1/2-inch-thick slices. Carefully transfer half of biscotti to second prepared baking sheet.

4. Arrange biscotti, cut sides down, on baking sheets. Bake for 15 minutes. Reduce heat to 200 degrees. Bake for 40 minutes, or until biscotti are dry. Cool completely (biscotti will harden as they cool).

Variation: Melt dark or white chocolate, then dip bottoms of biscotti into chocolate to coat. Transfer biscotti to waxed paper; set aside until chocolate becomes firm.

Anjelica Huston wears many hats—actor, director, and producer—so it comes as no surprise that she's been known to don a chef's hat as well. From cooking one-pot meals like soup for her husband, sculptor Robert Graham, to indulging them both with grab-and-go treats, Anjelica knows that the secret to having it all is to keep it simple, especially in the kitchen. These quick cookies are a multitasker's delight—as tasty with coffee for breakfast as they are for a midday—or midnight—snack.

Check out Anjelica's Academy Award®-winning performance in **Prizzi's Honor** or her wickedly funny turn in **The Addams Family**.

Anjelica Huston's Having-It-All Caramel Shortbread

makes 16 pieces **prep time** 15 minutes

1	box (5.3-ounce) pure butter shortbread triangles, *Walkers*®
20	soft caramel candies, unwrapped, *Brach's Milk Maid*®
1	tablespoon whole milk
½	cup chopped walnuts, toasted
1	cup semisweet chocolate morsels, *Nestlé*®

1. Line cookie sheet with parchment paper. Place shortbread triangles on cookie sheet, spacing evenly apart.

2. Combine caramels and milk in small microwavable bowl. Melt in microwave on medium power for 1½ minutes, stirring every 30 seconds, or until smooth. Drizzle melted caramel over shortbread. Cool caramel slightly, then sprinkle with walnuts. Gently press walnuts into caramel.

3. Melt chocolate morsels in microwave on medium power for 2½ minutes, stirring every 30 seconds, or until melted and smooth. Dip shortbread into melted chocolate, covering half of each shortbread. Set shortbread aside on prepared cookie sheet until chocolate is firm. Store in airtight container at room temperature.

Variation: Substitute the semisweet chocolate morsels with premier white morsels. Dip half of the shortbread cookies in melted white morsels for two varieties.

Queen Latifah is a sweet surprise. In the film **Chicago**, her silky smooth voice is an unexpected treat, as is her commitment to mentoring young girls. Even her name is a revelation—Latifah means delicate and sensitive in Arabic. These charming little cakes are another delicious discovery, with a delicacy and sweet surprise all their own. The apricot is baked on the bottom—just flip them over to reveal the delightful fruit center. They're soft, sweet, and soothing, just like our Queen L.

See Grammy®-winner Queen Latifah in the film **Bringing Down the House** (she was executive producer, too) or catch her Academy Award®-nominated performance in **Chicago**.

Queen Latifah's Silky Smooth Apricot Mini Cakes

makes 36 mini cakes **prep time** 20 minutes
baking time 15 minutes **cooling time** 15 minutes

- **36** dried apricots, **Sunsweet®**
- **4** ounces cream cheese, room temperature, **Philadelphia®**
- **3** tablespoons powdered sugar
- **½** cup finely chopped walnuts, toasted
- **1** box (18.25-ounce) classic yellow cake mix, **Duncan Hines Moist Deluxe®**
- **1⅓** cups water
- **⅓** cup vegetable oil
- **3** eggs
- **2** teaspoons pure almond extract, **McCormick®**
  Additional powdered sugar (optional)

Special Equipment
3 mini-cupcake pans (12 cups each)
  Pastry bag (without decorator's tip)

1. Preheat oven to 350 degrees F. Butter and flour three 12-cup mini-cupcake pans.

2. Using kitchen shears, cut ¼-inch piece off 1 end of each apricot. Insert handle of wooden spoon into slit of each apricot to form pocket; set aside.

3. Beat cream cheese in large bowl until light and fluffy. Beat in 3 tablespoons powdered sugar. Mix in walnuts. Spoon cream cheese mixture into pastry bag without decorator's tip. Pipe cream cheese mixture into pockets of prepared apricots. Place 1 filled apricot in each cup of prepared mini-cupcake pans. Combine cake mix, water, oil, eggs, and almond extract in large bowl. Beat for 2 minutes or until well blended. Spoon 1 tablespoon of batter over each apricot in pans.

4. Bake for 15 minutes or until lightly golden. Cool cakes completely in pans on cooling racks. Arrange cakes, apricot sides up, on serving platter. Dust with additional powdered sugar (optional).

Flamboyant funnyman Nathan Lane has mastered stage, screen, and television. What's next? The kitchen! **The Man Who Came to Dinner** star has a soft spot for dessert, especially ice cream fried to a delectable crunch. This sumptuous scene stealer is a fiesta of flavors—warm and crispy on the outside, cool and creamy on the inside. Serve it in a tall, cool parfait glass for a south-of-the-border treat just north of nirvana.

If you missed Nathan's Tony Award®-winning act in **The Producers**, you can view his classic comic turns in **The Birdcage** and **Mouse Hunt**.

Nathan Lane's Fabulous Fried Ice Cream

servings 4 **prep time** 15 minutes
freezing time 4 hours **cooking time** 4 minutes

1	quart vanilla ice cream, *Häagen-Dazs*®
5	cups honey crunch cornflakes, *Kellogg's*®
2	teaspoons ground cinnamon, *McCormick*®
2	eggs
	Canola oil for frying
4	tablespoons honey, *Sue Bee*®
¹/₂	cup frozen whipped topping, thawed, *Cool Whip*® (optional)

1. Scoop 8 balls of ice cream and place ¹/₂ inch apart on cookie sheet. Freeze for 3 hours or until ice cream is frozen solid.

2. Combine cornflakes and cinnamon in large resealable plastic bag; seal bag. Using rolling pin, crush cornflakes into crumbs. Transfer crumb mixture to large bowl. Removing 1 ice cream ball at a time from freezer, roll ice cream balls in crumb mixture, pressing crumbs onto ice cream to coat completely. Freeze ice cream balls until frozen solid.

3. Beat eggs in medium bowl to blend. Working with 1 ice cream ball at a time, dip balls into eggs, turning to coat, then roll balls in crumb mixture, pressing crumb mixture to coat ice cream balls again. Return ice cream balls to freezer.

4. To fry ice cream balls, add enough oil to large deep saucepan to come halfway up sides of pan. Heat oil over medium-high heat to about 300 degrees F. Using fryer basket or slotted spoon, add 2 ice cream balls to hot oil. Fry for 1 minute, or just until coating is crisp. Using slotted spoon, remove ice cream balls from oil and place on paper towel to drain excess oil. Transfer ice cream balls to dessert dish or cup. Drizzle with 1 tablespoon of honey and dollop with whipped topping (optional). Serve immediately. Repeat frying with remaining ice cream balls.

Style, grace, glamour—Sharon Stone has them all. The toast of Tinseltown, ever elegant Sharon, a devoted mom, has shifted her priorities to focus on the sweeter side of life—life with young sons Roan and Laird. For a dessert that sizzles with style, Sharon chooses this luxuriously luscious layer cake. It's the stuff of fantasy—layer upon layer of sweetly sensual chocolate and white cake, stacked with stripes of fluffy frosting in between and crowned with curls of rich white chocolate. It's a divine diva of a dessert—a dream to make … and serve.

See Sharon sizzle in her Oscar®-nominated role in **Casino** and her romantic romp in **The Muse**. You can also see Sharon's layered performance in **Cold Creek Manor**.

Sharon Stone's Sexy Sweet Chocolate Layer Cake

servings 12 to 14 **prep time** 10 minutes **baking time** 30 minutes **cooling time** 30 minutes **frosting time** 25 minutes

1	box (18.25-ounce) Swiss chocolate cake mix, *Duncan Hines Moist Deluxe*®
2^1/2	cups water
1	cup vegetable oil
6	eggs
1	box (18.25-ounce) classic white cake mix, *Duncan Hines Moist Deluxe*®
1	container (16-ounce) rich and creamy dark chocolate frosting, *Betty Crocker Rich & Creamy*®
2	containers (12 ounces each) fluffy white frosting, *Betty Crocker Whipped*®
	Chocolate Curls: 1 bar (8-ounce) white chocolate, *Lindt*® (optional)

1. Preheat oven to 350 degrees F. Butter and flour four 8-inch round cake pans.

2. Combine chocolate cake mix, 1^1/4 cups of the water, ^{1}/2 cup of the oil, and 3 of the eggs in large bowl. Beat for 2 minutes or until well blended. Divide batter between 2 prepared cake pans.

3. Combine the white cake mix, the remaining 1^1/4 cups water, ^{1}/2 cup oil, and 3 eggs in another large bowl. Beat for 2 minutes or until well blended. Divide batter between the remaining 2 prepared cake pans. Bake the 4 cakes for 30 minutes or until toothpick inserted into centers of cakes comes out clean.

4. Cool cakes in pans on cooling rack for 15 minutes. Invert cakes onto cooling rack. Cool cakes completely. Using sharp or serrated knife, cut each cake horizontally in half, forming 8 layers total. Place 1 white cake layer, cut side down, on platter; spread ^{1}/4 cup of dark chocolate frosting over top of cake. Place 1 chocolate cake layer, cut side up, on top of first cake layer; spread ^{1}/4 cup of white frosting over top of chocolate cake layer. Repeat layering and frosting until all layers are used. Frost entire cake with remaining white frosting. Top with Chocolate Curls (optional). Refrigerate cake until ready to serve.

To make optional Chocolate Curls: Chocolate bars must be at room temperature. Using vegetable peeler, scrape 1 long side of chocolate bars, forming curls.

On HBO's **Sex and the City**, Kristin Davis is known as the "sweet" one. Savvy on the show, she's equally savvy with a spatula. She grew up in the South, where baking is highly regarded as art, and her baking skills were definitely appreciated on the set. Like Kristin—and her TV alter ego Charlotte—this simply divine angel food cake is the epitome of cool elegance. Add a halo of fresh mint, and it's positively heaven sent.

Spend a fun night with Kristin on HBO's **Sex and the City**, now on TBS and DVD.

Kristin Davis' Savvy-Simple Lime Whip Angel Food

servings 6 to 8 **prep time** 10 minutes
cooling time 15 minutes **chilling time** 1 hour

1 purchased (12-ounce) angel food cake
1 cup boiling water
1 box (3-ounce) lime gelatin dessert mix, *Jell-O*®
1 cup cold whole milk
1 box (3.4-ounce) cheesecake-flavored instant pudding and pie filling mix, *Jell-O*®
3 tablespoons lime juice, *ReaLime*®
1½ cups frozen whipped topping, thawed, *Cool Whip*®
Fresh mint sprigs (optional)

1. Place angel food cake on serving platter. Using wooden or metal skewer, pierce 3-inch-deep holes all over top of cake.

2. Combine 1 cup of boiling water and the lime gelatin mix in large bowl; stir until gelatin dissolves. Cool slightly (do not add cold water). Carefully pour ¼ cup of warm dissolved gelatin over cake, allowing it to sink into holes. Refrigerate cake.

3. Add milk and instant pudding mix to remaining dissolved gelatin in bowl. Whisk until smooth; whisk in lime juice. Refrigerate for 30 minutes or until lime mixture thickens to pudding consistency. Using large rubber spatula, fold whipped topping into lime mixture. Refrigerate lime whip for 30 minutes. Spread lime whip all over cake. Refrigerate until ready to serve. Garnish with mint sprigs (optional).

Note: This cake is best eaten within 3 days.

Balanced meals—and a balanced life—get top billing at the Edwardses' house, where superdad Anthony puts parenting on the front burner. While wife, Jeanine Lobell, founder and chairman of Stila Cosmetics, keeps stars such as Nicole Kidman, Cameron Diaz, and Julianne Moore looking beautiful, Anthony keeps their own brood of three happy with nutritious noshes, like these clever little cream cheese-filled sandwiches. They're baked in an aluminum juice can. Busy dads and moms: Simply slice, fill, and serve.

Miss Anthony on **E.R.**? Rent his latest films **The Forgotten** and **Northfork,** or travel back in time to catch his not-to-be-missed roles in **Top Gun** and **Fast Times at Ridgemont High** (Anthony's film debut).

Anthony Edwards' Superdad Banana Nut Sandwiches

makes 6 large or 24 bite-size sandwiches **prep time** 10 minutes
baking time 1 hour **cooling time** 30 minutes **frosting time** 10 minutes

$1/2$ **cup chopped walnuts, toasted**
**2 boxes (13.9 ounces each) banana quick bread mix,
    Betty Crocker®**
$1^1/2$ **cups water**
4 eggs
$1/3$ **cup vegetable oil**
$3/4$ **cup cream cheese frosting, Betty Crocker Rich & Creamy®**

Special Equipment
**1 can (46-ounce, such as from Dole® pineapple juice), cleaned,
    dried, and with one end of can removed**

1. Position rack in lower third of oven to allow enough space for can to stand upright. Preheat oven to 350 degrees F. Generously butter inside of can.

2. Toss walnuts with 1 tablespoon of banana bread mix in small bowl to coat. Combine remaining bread mix, water, eggs, and oil in large bowl. Beat for 2 minutes or until well blended. Stir in walnut mixture. Transfer batter to prepared can.

3. Bake for 1 hour or until skewer inserted into center of bread comes out clean. Cool bread in pan on cooling rack for 20 minutes. Run knife around can sides to loosen bread; invert bread onto cooling rack. Cool bread completely.

4. Cut bread crosswise into twelve $1/2$-inch-thick slices. Spread 1 tablespoon of frosting over 1 bread slice. Top with another bread slice. Repeat with remaining frosting and bread slices. Serve sandwiches whole or cut each sandwich into 4 wedges to make 24 bite-size sandwiches. Arrange sandwiches on serving platter.

Variation: Coarsely mash two fresh ripe bananas into the cream cheese frosting for a satisfying filling.

A flighty flight attendant in **Airplane!**, a yuppie dropout in **Lost in America**, and a dysfunctional shrink's wife in **What About Bob?**, Julie Hagerty is not an actress to be trifled with. On-screen or onstage, Juilliard-trained Julie's roles are always memorable—much like this pretty pound cake trifle. Triangles of rich, buttery pound cake are delectably doused in sweet sherry and layered in a glass bowl with mixed berries, pudding, and whipped topping, then chilled to crowd-pleasing perfection. In spring or summer, swap orange or pineapple juice for the sherry for a cool and creamy tropical treat.

Watch Julie shine on Broadway (she's received both the Los Angeles Drama Critics Award and the Theatre World Award) or view her on the silver screen in films such as **A Guy Thing**.

Julie Hagerty's Perfect Pound Cake Trifle

servings 8 to 10 **prep time** 15 minutes **chilling time** 15 minutes

1   frozen pound cake (10.75-ounce), thawed, *Sara Lee*®
1/2   cup cream sherry, *Harveys Bristol Cream*®
2   bags (12 ounces each) frozen mixed berries, thawed and drained
3   cups cold whole milk
1   box (5.1-ounce) vanilla instant pudding and pie filling mix, *Jell-O*®
1   container (12-ounce) frozen whipped topping, thawed, *Cool Whip*®

1. Trim crusts off pound cake and cut cake crosswise into 3/4-inch-thick slices. Cut each cake slice diagonally in half, forming triangles. Place pound cake triangles in bottom of 2 1/2-quart clear-glass bowl. Brush pound cake generously with sherry. Spoon mixed berries evenly over cake.

2. Whisk milk and pudding mix in large bowl for 2 minutes or until creamy and beginning to thicken. Refrigerate pudding for 5 minutes or until pudding thickens. Pour pudding over mixed berries.

3. Refrigerate trifle for 10 minutes. Spread whipped topping over trifle. Cover with plastic wrap and refrigerate until ready to serve.

Note: This dessert tastes even better when served the next day.

Light & Healthy Treats

I try to eat healthy, but I have a relentless sweet tooth. I know it's a little naughty and I know I should feel a bit guilty, but I don't. You only live once and you deserve a treat. But as with so much in life, less is more.

I have a pair of jeans I call my "check jeans." If I can't fit in these jeans, it's time to cut back. Luckily, cutting back on calories doesn't mean cutting back on taste. Every one of these desserts is a personal favorite, irresistibly rich and creamy and soothingly satisfying, and I never feel like I'm missing a thing. From refreshing fruit to deep, dark chocolate, they're the ultimate in easy indulgence—a luscious way to start the day, a quick burst for the afternoon blahs, or a bedtime snack that invites sweet dreams. From cookies and creams to puddings and cakes, there's a dessert for every desire—whether you're dieting or not!

The Recipes

Perfectly Peachy Sorbet

servings 8 **prep time** 10 minutes
chilling time 30 minutes **freezing time** 2 hours
calories 40 **fat** 0 grams **saturated fat** 0 grams **cholesterol** 0 milligrams

- ³/₄ cup peach pie filling, *Comstock More Fruit*®
- 1 tablespoon sugar-free low-calorie peach-flavored gelatin dessert mix, *Jell-O*®
- 1 cup boiling water
- 1½ cups peach nectar, chilled, *Kerns*®

Special Equipment
  1-quart ice cream maker

1. Puree peach pie filling in blender until smooth. Set aside.

2. In mixing bowl, stir peach-flavored gelatin into boiling water until dissolved (about 2 minutes). When gelatin is completely dissolved, stir in chilled peach nectar and pureed pie filling until blended. Cover with plastic wrap and cool in refrigerator for 30 minutes.

3. Pour peach mixture into 1-quart ice cream maker and freeze according to manufacturer's instructions. When sorbet is frozen, transfer to airtight container and freeze for at least 2 hours*.

*Note: Sorbet freezes very hard—let sit at room temperature for 5 minutes before trying to scoop.

Really Raspberry Sorbet

servings 8 **prep time** 15 minutes
chilling time 30 minutes **freezing time** 2 hours
calories 12 **fat** 0 grams **saturated fat** 0 grams **cholesterol** 0 milligrams

- ³/₄ cup frozen raspberries, thawed and drained
- 1 tablespoon sugar-free low-calorie raspberry-flavored gelatin dessert mix, *Jell-O*®
- ¹/₃ cup no-calorie sweetener, *Splenda*®
- 1 cup boiling water
- 1¹/₃ cups low-carb cranberry-raspberry juice, chilled

Special Equipment
  1-quart ice cream maker

1. Puree raspberries in blender until smooth. Push puree through fine mesh strainer to remove seeds. Set aside.

2. In mixing bowl, stir raspberry-flavored gelatin and no-calorie sweetener into boiling water until dissolved (about 2 minutes). When gelatin is completely dissolved, stir in chilled cranberry-raspberry juice and pureed raspberries until blended. Cover with plastic wrap and cool in refrigerator for 30 minutes.

3. Pour raspberry mixture into 1-quart ice cream maker and freeze according to manufacturer's instructions. When sorbet is frozen, transfer to airtight container and freeze for at least 2 hours*.

Luscious Lemon-Lime Sorbet

servings 8 **prep time** 10 minutes
chilling time 30 minutes **freezing time** 2 hours
calories 66 **fat** 0 grams **saturated fat** 0 grams **cholesterol** 0 milligrams

- 1 tablespoon sugar-free low-calorie lime-flavored gelatin dessert mix, *Jell-O*®
- 1 cup boiling water
- 1 cup cold water
- 1 cup frozen lemonade concentrate, thawed

Special Equipment
  1-quart ice cream maker

1. In mixing bowl, stir lime-flavored gelatin into boiling water until dissolved (about 2 minutes). When gelatin is completely dissolved, stir in cold water and lemonade concentrate until blended. Cover with plastic wrap and cool in refrigerator for 30 minutes.

2. Pour lemon mixture into 1-quart ice cream maker and freeze according to manufacturer's instructions. When sorbet is frozen, transfer to airtight container and freeze for at least 2 hours*.

Grilled Pineapple with Iced Coconut Cream

servings 8 **prep time** 20 minutes
freezing time 2 hours
grilling time 10 minutes
assembly time 5 minutes

calories 134 **fat** 3 grams **saturated fat** 2 grams **cholesterol** 3 milligrams

Iced Coconut Cream
2   cups piña colada yogurt (99% fat-free), *Yoplait Original*®
1   can (11.5-ounce) pineapple-coconut nectar, *Kerns*®
1   teaspoon rum extract, *McCormick*®

Grilled Pineapple
1   fresh pineapple
¼   cup sweetened shredded coconut, lightly toasted*, *Baker's*®

Special Equipment
   1-quart ice cream maker

Iced Coconut Cream
1. Stir together yogurt, nectar, and rum extract in mixing bowl. Pour into 1-quart ice cream maker and freeze according to manufacturer's directions. When coconut cream is frozen, transfer to airtight container and freeze for at least 2 hours.

Grilled Pineapple
2. Remove top, bottom, and outer layer of pineapple. Slice pineapple into 8 rings. With small knife, cut out core of each slice.

3. In grill pan over high heat (or on outdoor grill), grill pineapple rings for 3 to 5 minutes. Turn over and grill for additional 3 to 5 minutes. Transfer slices to plate; set aside.

4. To assemble, place pineapple ring on plate with scoop of Iced Coconut Cream. Top with any accumulated juice from pineapple. Sprinkle with toasted coconut.

*****Tip:** To toast shredded coconut, preheat oven to 350 degrees F. Place coconut on cookie sheet. Toast for 6 to 8 minutes or until coconut turns light brown.

Note: Iced Coconut Cream freezes hard—let sit at room temperature for 5 minutes before trying to scoop.

Triple Orange Angel Food Cake

servings 12 **prep time** 10 minutes
baking time 40 minutes
cooling time 2 hours **frosting time** 5 minutes

calories 181 **fat** 0 grams **saturated fat** 0 grams **cholesterol** 0 milligrams

1	can (15-ounce) mandarin oranges in light syrup, *Geisha®*
	Water
1	box (16-ounce) angel food cake mix, *Betty Crocker®*
1	tablespoon orange zest
1	container (8-ounce) fat-free frozen whipped topping, thawed, *Cool Whip Free®*

1. Lower rack in oven to bottom rung. Preheat oven to 350 degrees F.

2. Drain mandarin oranges, reserving syrup in measuring cup. Set oranges aside. Add enough water to the reserved syrup to make 1¼ cups; set aside. Measure out 1 cup of mandarin oranges; reserve remaining oranges for garnish.

3. In large mixing bowl, combine angel food cake mix, syrup–water mixture, and orange zest. With electric mixer, beat on low speed for 30 seconds. Scrape down sides of bowl and beat on medium speed for 1 minute.

4. Pour batter into ungreased angel food tube pan. Carefully place the 1 cup orange segments around top of cake batter. Bake for 40 minutes or until top of cake is cracked and dark golden brown. Remove cake from oven and invert pan onto glass bottle. Cool 2 hours.

5. When completely cool, remove cake from pan and frost with whipped topping. Garnish with reserved orange segments.

Note: Avoid excessive stirring of fat-free whipped topping as it may become watery.

Ruby Grapefruit and Mint Granita

servings 8 **prep time** 5 minutes
freezing time 5 hours

calories 56 **fat** 0 grams **saturated fat** 0 grams **cholesterol** 0 milligrams

- 4 cups refrigerated ruby red grapefruit juice from concentrate
- 2 teaspoons honey, *Sue Bee*®
- 2 tablespoons finely chopped fresh mint leaves
  Fresh mint sprigs, for garnish

1. In mixing bowl, combine the grapefruit juice, honey, and chopped mint. Pour into 13×9-inch glass pan and freeze for at least 4 hours.

2. When granita is frozen, remove from freezer. With tines of fork, "scrape" granita to create icy flakes. Place granita back into freezer for 1 hour. Spoon granita into bowls or parfait glasses and garnish with sprigs of fresh mint.

Note: Granita is a refreshing Italian frozen mixture of water, sugar, and liquid flavoring such as fruit juice, wine, or coffee.

Watermelon Skewers with Citrus Feta

makes 24 skewers **prep time** 15 minutes
marinating time overnight
assembly time 10 minutes

calories 122 **fat** 12 grams **saturated fat** 3 grams **cholesterol** 8 milligrams

- 8 ounces mild feta cheese, *Athenos*®
  Zest of 1 lemon
- 2 tablespoons peppercorns, crushed, *McCormick*®
- 1 cup olive oil
- 4 cups cubed ($3/4$-inch cubes) seedless watermelon
- $1^1/2$ cups green olives, *Lindsay*®
- 24 6-inch bamboo skewers

1. Slice feta cheese into $1/2$-inch cubes. In small bowl, combine feta, lemon zest, crushed peppercorns, and olive oil; toss gently. Marinate in the refrigerator overnight.

2. To assemble, thread watermelon cubes, feta cheese, and olives alternately on skewers. Drizzle remaining marinade over skewers and serve.

Banana
Pudding Bites

servings 8 **prep time** 15 minutes
chilling time 3 hours

Banana pudding is the house dessert of the South. This elegant, bite-size version boasts the same silky flavor but is downscaled for dessert trays, picnic boxes, or individual servings. **Warning:** Nobody can eat just one!

calories 185 **fat** 5 grams **saturated fat** 1 gram **cholesterol** 0 milligrams

3 ripe bananas, peeled
32 vanilla wafer cookies, *Nabisco Nilla Wafers®*
1 cup prepared* fat-free sugar-free instant reduced-calorie banana cream pudding and pie filling mix, *Jell-O®*
4 vanilla wafer cookies, crumbled, *Nabisco Nilla Wafers®*

1. Remove the ends from peeled bananas and discard. Cut each banana into ten to twelve ½-inch slices.

2. Place vanilla wafer cookies on platter; top each cookie with a banana piece. Dollop a heaping teaspoon of pudding over each banana piece. Sprinkle with crumbled cookies to garnish.

*** To prepare pudding:** In a bowl, whisk together 1 box (3.4-ounce) banana cream pudding mix and 1½ cups fat-free milk for 2 minutes. Cover with plastic wrap and refrigerate for 3 hours.

Bake Sale

Stephanie calling her girlfriend for fast bake sale backup.

HELPFUL HINTS, TIPS, AND TRICKS

PACKAGING ITEMS FOR SALE: Your local grocery store has many packaging ideas for your bake sale items. Disposable foil baking pans—especially the mini-loaf pans—are great. You can also use decorative disposable plastic containers. Another attractive alternative: Buy inexpensive cake pans at your local discount store. You can sell the items right in the pans!

MORE PACKAGING IDEAS: Wrap items in clear cellophane rather than plastic wrap for a more professional look. Tie packages with raffia or make your own ribbon by cutting inexpensive fabric with pinking shears.

SIGNS, LABELS, AND TAGS: Use pinking shears or other decorating scissors to cut out signs, labels, or price tags for your baked items. Use a hole punch and a piece of raffia or ribbon to attach tags to your items. For a fresh homebaked look, use brown butcher paper and twine.

NOTE: Please read each and every chapter opener as there are numerous helpful hints, tips, and tricks to know for fast, fabulous results when making a delicious Semi-Homemade® dessert.

The Recipes

Aunt Sandy helps set up a bake sale with Austen, Stephanie, Danielle, and Brycer

Cherry Lollipops

makes 20 lollipops
prep time 10 minutes

These hard candy lollipops are the perfect project for pint-size chefs. Make them in any color or flavor you want—even in fun shapes, using metal cookie cutters or candy molds, available at most kitchen stores. To make cute gifts, holiday treats, or party favors, tie colorful ribbons around the sticks and curl the ends by pulling the ribbons between your thumb and the blade of a pair of scissors.

Nonstick cooking spray, *PAM*®
¾ **cup granulated sugar**
½ **cup light corn syrup, *Karo*®**
¼ **cup butter**
1 **box (3-ounce) cherry-flavored gelatin dessert mix, *Jell-O*®**

Special Equipment
20 4-inch lollipop sticks
Candy thermometer
Metal tablespoon-size measuring spoon

1. Spray 2 large cookie sheets with cooking spray. Arrange 10 lollipop sticks on each baking sheet, spacing evenly apart.

2. Stir sugar, corn syrup, and butter in small saucepan over low heat until sugar has dissolved. Slowly bring to boil, stirring frequently. Continue cooking for 7 minutes or until candy thermometer registers 275 degrees F. Add gelatin and stir until smooth.

3. Using metal tablespoon and working quickly, spoon syrup over one end of each lollipop stick. Cool completely. Remove lollipops from cookie sheets and wrap each lollipop in plastic wrap. Store in airtight container.

Hobo S'Mores

makes 36 pieces **prep time** 30 minutes
chilling time 1 hour

Hobos big and small will go coco-loco over these deliciously dippable S'Mores on a stick. Dunk them in warm chocolate, then roll in nuts, granola, fruit, or candy sprinkles for a slam dunk of a snack.

36 large marshmallows, *Kraft Jet-Puffed*®
1 container (16-ounce) dark chocolate frosting,
   Betty Crocker Rich & Creamy®
1$\frac{1}{2}$ cups graham cracker crumbs, *Nabisco Honey Maid*®
1$\frac{1}{2}$ cups semisweet chocolate mini morsels, *Nestlé*®

Special Equipment
36 lollipop sticks or frozen pop sticks

1. Line cookie sheet with waxed paper. Insert lollipop stick into one end of each marshmallow.

2. Microwave frosting for 30 seconds or just until frosting feels warm to touch. Dip 1 marshmallow at a time into frosting, allowing excess to drip off.

3. Dip bottom of marshmallow (the end without the stick) and one side of marshmallow into graham cracker crumbs. Dip opposite side of marshmallow into mini morsels.

4. Stand, flat ends down, on prepared cookie sheet. Serve immediately or refrigerate for 1 hour.

Fruit Pizza Pie

servings 8 to 10 **prep time** 10 minutes
baking time 20 minutes **cooling time** 45 minutes

Turn your kitchen into a pizzeria with a piece of creative cookery the whole gang will enjoy. Easy make-and-bake pizza pies make a scrumptious snack for a birthday party, family night, or weekend get-together. Set up a topping bar, pat out cookie-dough crusts, and let the kids top their own personal pizzas with their favorite fruit toppings. Cut in individual portions to sell at neighborhood bake sales.

1	package (18-ounce) refrigerated sugar cookie dough, *Pillsbury®*
1	container (8-ounce) cream cheese, *Philadelphia®*
2	tablespoons granulated sugar
1	teaspoon pure vanilla extract, *McCormick®*
¼	cup seedless red raspberry jam
2	kiwifruits, peeled and sliced
6	canned peach halves, drained, patted dry, thinly sliced, *Del Monte®*
¼	cup fresh raspberries, blueberries, or chopped strawberries
2	tablespoons sweetened flaked coconut, toasted, *Baker's®*

1. Preheat oven to 375 degrees F. Roll cookie dough into ball, then press into shallow round pizza pan or 9-inch round cake pan. Bake for 20 minutes or until golden brown. Cool crust completely in pan on cooling rack, about 45 minutes.

2. Combine cream cheese, sugar, and vanilla in large bowl. Beat for 3 minutes or until light and fluffy. Spread cream cheese mixture over crust. Spread jam over cream cheese mixture. Decorate with kiwi slices, peaches, raspberries, and toasted coconut.

Chocolate Lover's Pizza Variation: Make crust with an 18-ounce roll of refrigerated chocolate chip cookie dough. Top with hot fudge topping, mini marshmallows, chocolate morsels, and toasted slivered almonds. Rewarm pizza in oven until marshmallows begin to melt.

Frosting Variation: A can of white frosting may be substituted for the cream cheese.

Cinnamon Sugar Crumble Cakes

makes 3 loaves
prep time 10 minutes
baking time 35 minutes

Nonstick cooking spray, *PAM*®
1/4 **cup instant coffee crystals, *Maxwell House*®**
2 **tablespoons hot water**
1 **box (21-ounce) cinnamon crumb cake mix, *Krusteaz*®**
1/2 **cup water**
1 **egg, beaten to blend**
2 **6-inch biscotti cookies, crushed**

Special Equipment
5³/₄×3¹/₄×2-inch disposable miniature loaf pans (3)

1. Preheat oven to 350 degrees F. Spray loaf pans with cooking spray.

2. In large bowl, stir together coffee crystals and the 2 tablespoons of hot water until granules dissolve. To bowl, add cake mix packet (reserve topping mixture for later), the 1/2 cup water, and the egg. Stir just until moistened (mixture will be lumpy); set aside.

3. Stir topping mixture and crushed biscotti in medium bowl.

4. Divide half of topping-biscotti mixture among the 3 prepared loaf pans. Spoon cake batter over topping mixture. Sprinkle remaining topping mixture over batter.

5. Bake for 35 minutes or until toothpick inserted into centers of loaves comes out clean. Serve warm or at room temperature.

Caramel Popcorn Cones

makes twelve 2-inch popcorn balls
prep time 20 minutes

18   soft caramel candies, unwrapped, *Brach's Milk Maid®*
2   tablespoons whole milk
¹/₂ cup finely chopped walnuts, toasted
1   package (3-ounce) microwave popcorn, popped,
       or about 4 cups popped popcorn, *Orville Redenbacher's®*

1. Line cookie sheet with waxed paper. Melt caramels with milk in microwave on low heat for 1¹/₂ minutes, stirring every 30 seconds, or until smooth. Stir walnuts into caramel mixture.

2. Using about ¹/₃ cup of popcorn for each ball, dip one end of each popcorn kernel into melted caramel and attach to another popcorn kernel. Repeat with remaining popcorn, forming twelve 2-inch popcorn balls. Store in airtight container at room temperature.

Double Decker Fudge

makes about 36 pieces
prep time 30 minutes **chilling time** 3 hours

4   cups semisweet chocolate morsels, *Nestlé®*
2   cans (14 ounces each) sweetened condensed
       milk, *Carnation®*
2   teaspoons pure vanilla extract, *McCormick®*
3   cups premier white morsels, *Nestlé®*

1. Line 8-inch square glass or metal baking pan with foil, allowing 2 inches of foil to hang over sides. Combine 3¹/₂ cups of the semisweet morsels, 2 cups of the condensed milk, and the vanilla in large glass bowl. Heat in microwave on medium power for 1¹/₂ minutes, stirring every 30 seconds or until melted and smooth.

3. Pour half of semisweet chocolate fudge mixture into prepared pan; smooth top with spatula. Immediately sprinkle ¹/₄ cup of the white morsels over fudge mixture. Let stand 30 seconds for morsels to melt slightly. Using toothpick or wooden skewer, swirl together to create marbled effect.

4. Combine 2¹/₂ cups of the white morsels and the remaining condensed milk in medium glass bowl. Heat in microwave on medium power for 2 minutes, stirring every 30 seconds or until melted and smooth.

5. Pour white fudge mixture over semisweet chocolate fudge mixture in pan; smooth top with spatula. Immediately sprinkle the remaining ¹/₂ cup of semisweet morsels over fudge. Let stand 30 seconds for morsels to melt slightly. Using a toothpick or a wooden skewer, swirl together to marble.

6. Pour remaining warm semisweet chocolate fudge over white fudge in pan; smooth top with spatula. Immediately sprinkle remaining ¹/₄ cup of white morsels over fudge. Refrigerate for at least 3 hours or until fudge is firm. Peel away foil and cut fudge into squares or desired shapes.

Rice Crispy Peanut Butter Treats

makes 36 treats **prep time** 5 minutes
chilling time 1 hour

3	cups crispy rice cereal, *Kellogg's Rice Krispies*®
1	cup extra crunchy peanut butter, *Jif*®
1	cup peanut butter chips, *Reese's*®
1	jar (7-ounce) marshmallow creme, *Kraft Jet-Puffed*®

1. Line cookie sheet with waxed paper. Using 2 wooden spoons, toss rice cereal, peanut butter, and peanut butter chips in large bowl to coat. Add marshmallow creme and toss until well combined.

2. Using 1-ounce cookie scoop, form mixture into 1^1/$_2$-inch balls. Place on prepared cookie sheet. Refrigerate for 1 hour or until firm. Store in airtight container.

Nutty Brittle

servings 30 **prep time** 5 minutes **cooking time** 10 minutes
cooling time 30 minutes **chilling time** 30 minutes

	Nonstick cooking spray, *PAM*®
24	soft caramel candies, unwrapped, *Brach's Milk Maid*®
^{3}/$_4$	cup toffee peanuts

1. Preheat oven to 200 degrees F. Line jelly roll pan with foil. Spray foil with cooking spray and place in preheated oven.

2. Spray heavy small saucepan with cooking spray. Add caramels and stir over low heat until melted. Stir in toffee peanuts and continue stirring for 5 minutes. Remove prepared pan from oven and quickly spread caramel-peanut mixture onto pan. Cool completely.

3. Cover pan with plastic wrap and refrigerate for 30 minutes. Break into bite-size pieces. Store in refrigerator.

Cookies

I learned to bake from scratch at my Grandma Lorraine's elbow. By the time I was eight, I was working my way through the *Better Homes and Gardens® red plaid cookbook* and *Joy of Cooking*, adding a pinch of this and a hint of that to make the recipes my own. Then, as now, baking relaxed me … giving me lots of home-and-hearth love to share.

Cookies are the ultimate comfort food, summoning up happy memories of a time when a gooey, warm-from-the-oven cookie could sweeten any day. It still can, whether you're 8 or 80! This chapter has all kinds of cookies for all kinds of tastes. There are old-fashioned cookies for the sentimental at heart and more sophisticated cookies for elegant celebrations. There are cookies for snacks and cookies for parties, even cookies to give as gifts. When I was young, I spent hours baking, but starting with store-bought dough lets you bake like a pro in a fraction of the time with all of the same fantastic flavor.

The Recipes

Basic Sugar Cookie Dough

makes 24 cookies **prep time** 25 minutes
baking time 8 minutes per batch

1   package (17.5-ounce) dry sugar cookie mix,
       Betty Crocker®
4   ounces cream cheese, softened, **Philadelphia®**
2   eggs
1   tablespoon vanilla extract or other flavoring, **McCormick®**
³/₄ to 1 cup all-purpose flour
       Flour, for dusting work surface

1. Preheat oven to 350 degrees F. In bowl of electric mixer, beat cookie mix with cream cheese until crumbly. Mix in eggs and vanilla until well combined.

2. Turn dough out onto a work surface and knead in up to 1 cup flour until dough is firm enough to roll out. For recipe variations (see recipes, pages 122, 124, and 133) stop at this point and proceed to step 1 of the desired recipe.

3. On a lightly floured surface, roll dough to ¹/₄-inch thickness. Cut out desired shapes. Place cookies 2 inches apart on ungreased cookie sheet and bake for 8 minutes or until edges are light golden brown. Cool on cooling rack.

Butter Rosettes

makes 48 cookies **prep time** 10 minutes
baking time 8 minutes per batch
frosting time 5 minutes

1   recipe Basic Sugar Cookie Dough (recipe, this page)
       Tubes of colored decorating frosting (with star tips)

Special Equipment
Cookie press with rosette template

1. Preheat oven to 350 degrees F. Prepare Basic Sugar Cookie Dough through step 2.

2. Put dough in cookie press fitted with a rosette template. Press dough 2 inches apart onto ungreased cookie sheet. Bake for 8 minutes or until edges are light golden brown. Cool completely on cooling rack.

3. Fit the tubes of decorating frosting with star tips. Decorate center of each cooled cookie with frosting rosette.

Peanut Butter Fudge Cookies

makes 36 cookies **prep time** 20 minutes
baking time 12 minutes per batch **frosting time** 5 minutes

1   package (18-ounce) refrigerated sugar cookie dough,
      room temperature, *Pillsbury*®
½ cup peanut butter, *Jif*®
1   can (16-ounce) chocolate frosting, *Pillsbury*®

Special Equipment
12-cup mini-cupcake pans (3)

1. Preheat oven to 350 degrees F. Lightly butter three 12-cup mini-cupcake pans.

2. Knead cookie dough and peanut butter just until swirled. Press about 1 rounded teaspoon of dough into each cup of prepared mini cupcake pans. Bake for 12 minutes or until cookies are light golden brown. Cool slightly in pan.

3. When slightly cool make indention in center of each cookie. Remove from pans to cooling rack. When completely cool, place about 1 teaspoon of frosting in center of each cookie.

Note: If desired, use a pastry bag fitted with a round tip to fill centers of cookies with chocolate frosting.

Checkerboard Cookies

makes 24 cookies
prep time 20 minutes **chilling time** 30 minutes
baking time 10 minutes per batch

1   recipe Basic Sugar Cookie Dough (recipe, page 122)
2   tablespoons unsweetened cocoa powder, *Hershey's*®
2   tablespoons semisweet mini chocolate morsels, *Nestlé*®

1. Prepare Basic Sugar Cookie Dough through step 2.

2. Divide dough into 3 equal pieces. Knead cocoa powder into one piece of dough and mini chocolate morsels into another.

3. Roll each of the 3 pieces of dough into a rope about ³/₄ inch in diameter. On ungreased cookie sheet, place 2 of the ropes parallel with sides touching and gently press the third onto top to form a triangle. Refrigerate for 30 minutes until dough is firm.

4. Preheat oven to 350 degrees. Slice dough into ½-inch-thick slices, and space 2 inches apart on ungreased cookie sheet. Bake for 10 minutes or until bottoms are golden brown. Cool on cooling rack.

Lemon Spritz Squares

makes 42 cookies **prep time** 25 minutes
freezing time 10 minutes
baking time 10 minutes per batch

1 package (17.5-ounce) dry sugar cookie mix, *Betty Crocker®*
4 ounces cream cheese, softened, *Philadelphia®*
1¼ cups all-purpose flour
¾ teaspoon lemon extract, *McCormick®*
2 eggs
1 tablespoon grated lemon zest
Flour, for dusting work surface
Powdered sugar, for garnishing

1. Preheat oven to 350 degrees F. In bowl of electric mixer, beat cookie mix and cream cheese until crumbly. Add flour in 3 parts, mixing well after each addition. Add lemon extract, eggs, and lemon zest; mix until just incorporated.

2. On lightly floured surface, roll out dough to 12×14-inch rectangle. Using fluted pastry cutter or sharp knife, cut dough into 2-inch squares.

3. Place squares 1 inch apart on ungreased cookie sheet. Freeze 10 minutes. Bake for 10 minutes or until bottoms are golden brown and tops are set. Cool completely on cooling rack. Dust with powdered sugar.

Glazed Doughnut Crisps

makes 16 cookies **prep time** 25 minutes
freezing time 10 minutes
baking time 12 minutes per batch

Doughnuts
1 package (18-ounce) refrigerated sugar cookie dough, room temperature, *Pillsbury®*
½ teaspoon brandy extract, *McCormick®*
½ cup all-purpose flour
Purchased vanilla frosting, *Pillsbury®*

Drippy Icing
1 cup powdered sugar, sifted
2 tablespoons milk
1 drop yellow food coloring

Doughnuts
1. Preheat oven to 350 degrees F. Cut cookie dough into 8 pieces. In bowl of electric mixer, thoroughly combine cookie dough pieces, brandy extract, and flour, adding flour in 2 parts. Divide dough into 16 pieces. Roll each piece into 6-inch rope.

2. Placing 2 inches apart on ungreased cookie sheet, shape each rope into ring-shaped doughnut, pinching ends together. Freeze for 10 minutes.

3. Bake for 12 minutes or until cookies are light golden brown. Cool completely on cooling rack. Frost each cookie with vanilla frosting. Drizzle Drippy Icing over cookies.

Drippy Icing
4. In small bowl, combine powdered sugar and milk. Tint with yellow food coloring. If necessary, add more powdered sugar to obtain desired consistency. Drizzle icing over cookies.

Snickerdoodles

makes 36 cookies **prep time** 15 minutes
baking time 10 minutes per batch

1   package (18-ounce) refrigerated sugar cookie dough,
     room temperature, *Pillsbury*®
2   ounces cream cheese, softened, *Philadelphia*®
1/2 cup powdered sugar
1   teaspoon vanilla extract or other flavoring, *McCormick*®
1/2 cup granulated sugar
1/4 teaspoon ground cinnamon, *McCormick*®

1. Preheat oven to 350 degrees F. Cut cookie dough into 8 pieces. In bowl of electric mixer, combine cookie dough pieces and cream cheese. Mix in powdered sugar and vanilla extract until dough is smooth.

2. Scoop dough by the tablespoon and roll into about 36 balls.

3. In a small bowl, combine granulated sugar and cinnamon. Roll balls in cinnamon-sugar mixture and place 2 inches apart on an ungreased cookie sheet. Bake for 10 minutes or until edges are light golden brown. Cool on cooling rack.

Oatmeal Date Spice Cookies

makes 36 cookies **prep time** 5 minutes
baking time 10 minutes per batch
cooling time 5 minutes

1   box (18.25-ounce) classic yellow cake mix, *Duncan Hines Moist Deluxe*®
1 1/2 sticks butter, melted
1/3 cup all-purpose flour
2   eggs
2   tablespoons pumpkin pie spice, *McCormick*®
2   teaspoons pure vanilla extract, *McCormick*®
1   cup quick-cooking oats, *Quaker Oats*®
1   cup chopped walnuts, toasted
1   cup chopped dates, *Sunsweet*®

1. Preheat oven to 375 degrees F. Combine cake mix, melted butter, flour, eggs, pumpkin pie spice, and vanilla in large bowl. Beat with an electric mixer for 1 minute or until well blended. Stir in oats, walnuts, and dates.

2. For each cookie, drop a heaping tablespoon of dough onto ungreased cookie sheet. Space cookies 2 inches apart. Bake for 10 minutes or until edges begin to brown slightly. Cool cookies on cookie sheet for 5 minutes. Transfer cookies to cooling rack to cool completely.

Note: To save time and effort, buy pre-chopped dates. If you need to chop your own, spray your knife or the blades of your food processor with nonstick cooking spray to minimize sticking.

White Peppermint Snowballs

makes 36 cookies **prep time** 20 minutes
baking time 8 minutes per batch

1 **package (18-ounce) refrigerated sugar cookie dough, room temperature, *Pillsbury*®**
1/3 **cup peppermint candies, crushed**
1 **cup powdered sugar**
Peppermint candies, crushed, for garnishing

1. Preheat oven to 350 degrees F. Cut cookie dough into 8 pieces. In bowl of electric mixer, thoroughly combine dough pieces, crushed peppermint candies, and 1/2 cup of the powdered sugar.

2. Roll dough into 1-inch diameter balls. Place 2 inches apart on ungreased cookie sheet. Bake for 8 minutes or until set. Cool slightly on cooling rack.

3. While still warm, roll cookies in the remaining 1/2 cup powdered sugar. Sprinkle with crushed peppermint candies.

Raspberry Windmill Cookies

makes 9 cookies **prep time** 25 minutes
chilling time 15 minutes **baking time** 12 minutes

1 **package (18-ounce) refrigerated sugar cookie dough, room temperature, *Pillsbury*®**
1/4 **cup cream cheese, *Philadelphia*®**
1/2 **teaspoon almond extract, *McCormick*®**
3 **tablespoons seedless raspberry jam**
9 **red candied cherry halves**

1. Preheat oven to 350 degrees F. Cut cookie dough into 8 pieces. In bowl of electric mixer, thoroughly combine cookie dough pieces, cream cheese, and almond extract. If dough is too soft, place in refrigerator for 15 minutes before using.

2. Roll dough out into 9×9-inch square. With sharp knife, cut dough into nine 3-inch squares. Move squares apart slightly so they are easier to work on.

3. Stir jam and spread about 1 teaspoon on each piece of dough. On each square, cut a slice from each corner almost to center.

4. Fold cut corner from each of 4 sides to center and press to hold it. In center of each cookie, add candied cherry half. Place on ungreased cookie sheet and bake for 12 minutes or until cookies are light golden brown. Cool on cooling rack.

White Chocolate Ornaments

makes 6 large cookies **prep time** 25 minutes
baking time 14 minutes

1 recipe **Basic Sugar Cookie Dough (see recipe, page 122)**
1 cup **white chocolate morsels, *Ghirardelli*®**
   Silver dragées in assorted sizes

1. Preheat oven to 350 degrees F. Prepare the Basic Sugar Cookie Dough through step 2, using 1 cup flour.

2. On lightly floured surface, roll dough out to 1/4- to 1/2-inch thickness. Using large ornament-shape cookie cutters, cut out 6 cookies. Place on ungreased cookie sheet. If desired, poke a hole in top of each cookie with a toothpick or skewer (if using as hanging ornaments). Bake for 14 minutes or until edges are light golden brown. Cool on cooling rack.

3. Line a cookie sheet with waxed paper. Melt white chocolate morsels in double boiler. Frost cookies with melted white chocolate. Decorate with drageés. Let stand on cookie sheet until set.

Cream Cheese Sugar Cutouts

makes 24 cookies **prep time** 20 minutes
baking time 10 minutes per batch

1 package **(18-ounce) refrigerated sugar cookie dough,**
   room temperature, *Pillsbury*®
3 ounces **cream cheese, softened, *Philadelphia*®**
3/4 cup **all-purpose flour**
1 teaspoon **vanilla extract, *McCormick*®**
   Flour, for dusting work surface
   Colored sugars, frosting, and candies

1. Preheat oven to 350 degrees F. Cut cookie dough into 8 pieces. In bowl of electric mixer, thoroughly combine dough pieces, cream cheese, flour, and vanilla. If dough is too soft, place in refrigerator for 15 minutes before using.

2. On a lightly floured surface, roll dough out to 1/4-inch thickness. Using your favorite cookie cutters, cut out cookies. Place on ungreased cookie sheets. If desired, sprinkle with colored sugar.

3. Bake for 10 minutes or until edges are light golden brown. Cool completely on cooling rack. Decorate as desired with colored sugars, frosting, and candies.

Candy Cane Twists

makes 24 cookies **prep time** 25 minutes
baking time 10 minutes per batch

1   package (18-ounce) refrigerated sugar cookie dough,
        room temperature, *Pillsbury®*
1/2   cup all-purpose flour
1/2   teaspoon peppermint extract, *McCormick®*
      Red food coloring

1. Preheat oven to 375 degrees F. Cut roll of cookie dough in half. Place halves in separate large mixing bowls. In one bowl, thoroughly mix 1/4 cup of the flour and the peppermint extract into cookie dough. In the second bowl, add the remaining 1/4 cup flour and enough food coloring to make dough red. Mix well.

2. Divide white and red dough into 24 pieces each (for a total of 48 pieces). Roll each piece into a rope 8 inches long and about 1/4 inch in diameter.

3. To shape candy canes, place one rope of each color side by side on an ungreased cookie sheets. Gently twist together and shape into candy cane. Repeat with remaining pieces, spacing cookies about 2 inches apart. Bake for 10 minutes or until edges are very lightly browned. Gently remove from cookie sheets and cool on cooling racks.

Gingerbread Snowflakes

makes 16 cookies **prep time** 20 minutes
baking time 8 minutes per batch

1   box (14.5-ounce) gingerbread mix, *Betty Crocker*®
¼   cup butter, melted
1   egg
¼   cup all-purpose flour, if needed
    Tubes of white decorating frosting
    Large crystal decorating sugar

1. Preheat oven to 350 degrees F. Lightly butter a cookie sheet. In bowl of electric mixer, combine gingerbread mix, melted butter, and egg until dough is smooth. If dough is too soft, add up to ¼ cup flour.

2. Roll out dough to ¼- to ½-inch thickness. Cut dough with a snowflake- or star-shape cookie cutter. Place cookies 2 inches apart on prepared cookie sheet and bake for 8 minutes or until set.

3. Cool completely on cooling rack. Decorate with tubes of white frosting and dust with crystal sugar.

Mint Wafers

makes 24 to 30 cookies **prep time** 20 minutes

2   bags (12 ounces each) semisweet chocolate
        morsels, *Nestlé*®
2   tablespoons butter or shortening
2   teaspoons peppermint extract, *McCormick*®
24 to 30 vanilla wafer cookies, *Nabisco Nilla Wafers*®

1. Place chocolate morsels and butter in small bowl. In two to three 30-second intervals, microwave chocolate and butter on 50 percent power, stirring after each interval. After chocolate and butter are completely melted and combined, stir in peppermint extract.

2. Place vanilla wafers on wire cooling rack over sheet of aluminum foil. Pour melted chocolate over each wafer, covering tops completely. Let cookies sit for 10 minutes or until chocolate is set.

Special Occasions

HELPFUL HINTS, TIPS, AND TRICKS

PARCHMENT PAPER: Parchment paper is a grease- and moisture-resistant paper with many culinary virtues. You can use it to make disposable pastry bags or line baking sheets for even cooking.

FONDANT: Ready-to-use rolled fondant is easy to work with and comes with step-by-step directions enclosed in the box. You can color white fondant any color. Drop liquid food coloring onto fondant a drop at a time, kneading the fondant until the desired color is achieved. It is best to wear disposable latex gloves to keep the color from staining your hands. You can find ready-to-use rolled fondant in cake decorating and hobby stores.

COLORING MARZIPAN: Color marzipan by kneading in liquid food coloring drop by drop. It is best to wear disposable latex gloves to keep the color from staining your hands.

LATEX GLOVES: These disposable gloves can be purchased in most grocery stores or shops that specialize in cake decorating.

NOTE: Please read each and every chapter opener as there are numerous helpful hints, tips, and tricks to know for fast, fabulous results when making a delicious Semi-Homemade® dessert.

The Recipes

Pink
Meringue Kisses

makes 24 cookies **prep time** 15 minutes
baking time 3 hours **cooling time** 20 minutes

3   **egg whites, at room temperature**
¼   **teaspoon cream of tartar, *McCormick*®**
¾   **cup granulated sugar**
1   **teaspoon imitation strawberry extract, *McCormick*®**
3   **drops red food coloring, *McCormick*®**

Special Equipment
   Pastry bag
   #4 star tip

1. Preheat oven to 200 degrees F. Line 2 heavy large cookie sheets with parchment paper.

2. Beat egg whites in clean large metal bowl on medium speed until foamy. Add cream of tartar. Increase speed to high and continue beating until soft peaks form. Gradually add sugar, 1 tablespoon at a time, beating until stiff peaks form, about 5 minutes. Quickly mix in strawberry extract. Stir in food coloring, 1 drop at a time, until desired color is achieved.

3. Spoon meringue into pastry bag fitted with star tip. Pipe twelve 1½-inch-high ×1½-inch-diameter mounds onto each prepared cookie sheet, spacing evenly apart. Bake for 3 hours or until dry and crisp. Cool meringues completely on baking sheets. Store in airtight container at room temperature.

White Meringues Variation: Omit the red food coloring and use 1 teaspoon white vanilla or ½ teaspoon white crème de cacao instead of the strawberry extract.

Mint Meringues Variation: Substitute ½ teaspoon mint extract or white crème de menthe and 2 to 3 drops green food coloring, adding slowly until the meringues are pale green.

Note: To ensure a completely smooth meringue, the sugar must be added a tablespoon at a time. When making meringues, it is very important to have any equipment (bowls, mixers, spatulas, spoons) scrupulously clean. Any grease or fat can wreck an egg white foam. If your meringues keep breaking, fat or grease could be the cause. Rub equipment with lemon juice, then rinse and dry completely to get rid of all traces of fat. Humidity is also a factor when making meringues. An old adage states never to make meringues on a damp day. It's true: When the sugar in meringues absorbs moisture, it turns soft and sticky.

Pastel Petit Fours

makes 12 petit fours
prep time 50 minutes

1 purchased (16-ounce) frozen pound cake, thawed, *Sara Lee*®
⅓ cup plus 2 tablespoons seedless red raspberry jam
1 tablespoon water
½ box (use 12 ounces) ready-to-use pure white rolled fondant, *Wilton*®
  Assorted food coloring (colors optional)
  Powdered sugar, for dusting work surface
½ cup fluffy white frosting, *Betty Crocker Whipped*®
12 sugar-coated jelly candies

Special Equipment
  Disposable latex gloves
  Pastry bag
  Small star tip

1. Using sharp knife, trim crust from cake. Cut cake crosswise into six 1½-inch-thick slices. Cut each slice vertically in half to make 12 pieces. Trim any uneven sides with sharp knife. Slice each cake piece in half and spread ½ teaspoon of jam over 6 pieces. Top with remaining cake pieces and set aside. To make glaze, whisk ⅓ cup of jam and water in small bowl until smooth. Brush raspberry glaze over tops and sides of cakes.

2. To decorate cakes, divide fondant into 6 pieces. Wearing gloves, knead different food coloring, 1 drop at a time, into each fondant piece until desired color is achieved. Divide each colored fondant piece in half. Sprinkle work surface and rolling pin with powdered sugar.

3. Roll out 1 fondant piece at a time into 5-inch diameter round that is ¼ inch thick, rotating to prevent sticking. Drape fondant over 1 prepared cake; smooth over surface. Trim excess fondant from around base of cake. Repeat with remaining cakes and fondant pieces. Spoon frosting into pastry bag fitted with star tip. Pipe frosting on top of cakes. Decorate with candies. Store in airtight container.

Variation: Use cookie cutters to cut cake slices into desired shapes.

Two-Tier Lemon Yellow Cake with Sugared Roses

servings 30 to 40 **prep time** 30 minutes
baking time 1 ½ hours **cooling time** 1 hour
chilling time 30 minutes **decorating time** 25 minutes

3   boxes (18.25 ounces each) lemon cake mix, *Betty Crocker SuperMoist®*
3¾ cups water
9   eggs
1   cup vegetable oil
1⅓ cups plus 2 tablespoons lemon curd, stirred to loosen, *Dickinson's®*
3   containers (12 ounces each) fluffy white or lemon frosting,
    Betty Crocker Whipped®

Special Equipment and Decorations
1   10-inch round cake pan with 3-inch sides
1   7-inch round cake pan with 3-inch sides
2   cardboard cake rounds (one 10-inch and one 7-inch)
2   12⅜-inch (⅜-inch diameter) plastic dowel rods, *Wilton®*
    Edible sugared roses or silk fabric roses

1. Preheat oven to 350 degrees F. Butter and flour cake pans. Combine 2 of the cake mixes, 2½ cups of water, 6 eggs, and ⅔ cup oil in large bowl. Beat for 3 minutes or until well blended. Transfer batter to 10-inch cake pan.

2. Combine the remaining cake mix, 1¼ cups water, 3 eggs, and ⅓ cup oil in the emptied large bowl used in step 1. Beat for 2 minutes or until well blended. Transfer batter to 7-inch cake pan.

3. Bake 7-inch cake for 1 hour and 10-inch cake for 1½ hours or until toothpick inserted into centers of cakes comes out clean. Cool cakes in pans on cooling racks for 20 minutes. Invert cakes onto cooling racks, remove pans, and cool completely.

4. To prepare layers, cut cakes horizontally in half. Place 1 tablespoon of lemon curd in center of each cardboard cake round. Place 10-inch cake top, cut side up, on top of 10-inch cardboard round. Spread 1 cup of curd over cake; top with 10-inch cake bottom, cut side down.

5. Place 7-inch cake top, cut side up, on top of 7-inch cardboard round. Spread ⅓ cup of curd over cake; top with 7-inch cake bottom, cut side down. Spread thin layer of frosting over cakes. Refrigerate until cold, about 30 minutes. Spread remaining frosting over cakes to coat completely. Using toothpick, swirl frosting decoratively.

6. To assemble, cut dowel rods crosswise into five 3-inch pieces. Place 10-inch cake on platter. Press 4 of the cut rods into cake, positioning about 3½ inches in from edge and spacing evenly. Press remaining rod into center. Place 7-inch cake on its cardboard on top of rods in 10-inch cake. Place sugared roses over cakes before serving.

Double Chocolate Cake with Chocolate Leaves

servings 18 **prep time** 25 minutes
baking time 35 minutes **cooling time** 1 hour
chilling time 20 minutes **decorating time** 25 minutes

Cake and Frosting
1   box (18.25-ounce) devil's food cake mix, *Duncan Hines Moist Deluxe®*
1⅓ cups water
½   cup vegetable oil
3   eggs
2   containers (16 ounces each) dark chocolate frosting,
      Betty Crocker Rich & Creamy®

Chocolate Leaves
½   cup semisweet chocolate morsels, *Nestlé®*
½   cup milk chocolate morsels, *Nestlé®*

Special Equipment and Decorations
1   9-inch-diameter round cake pan with 3-inch-high sides
1   6-inch-diameter round cake pan with 3-inch-high sides
20 lemon leaves, washed and dried well

Cake and Frosting
1. Preheat oven to 350 degrees F. Butter and flour cake pans. Combine cake mix, water, oil, and eggs in large bowl. Beat for 3 minutes or until well blended. Divide batter evenly between prepared pans. Bake for 35 minutes or until toothpick inserted into centers of cakes comes out clean. Cool cakes in pans on cooling racks for 15 minutes. Invert cakes onto cooling racks, remove pans, and cool completely.

2. To decorate, slice each cake horizontally in half. Place 9-inch cake top, cut side up, on serving platter. Spread ½ cup of frosting over cake; top with 9-inch cake bottom, cut side down. Place 6-inch cake top, cut side up, on platter. Spread ¼ cup of frosting over cake; top with 6-inch cake bottom, cut side down. Frost cakes with remaining frosting. Refrigerate for 20 minutes.

Chocolate Leaves
3. Line cookie sheet with parchment or waxed paper. Melt each kind of chocolate in a double boiler until smooth. Using a spatula, spread undersides of 10 leaves with melted semisweet chocolate. Spread the undersides of the other 10 leaves with the melted milk chocolate. Place leaves, chocolate sides up, on prepared cookie sheet. Do not allow chocolate to drip over leaf edges. Refrigerate until set, then peel away each leaf. Place 6-inch cake on top of 9-inch cake. Arrange chocolate leaves decoratively around sides of cakes.

Three-Tier White Cake with Raspberry Filling

servings: 40 to 50 **prep time** 1 hour
baking time 1½ hours **cooling time** 1 hour
chilling time 1 hour **decorating time** 1½ hours

3 **boxes (18.25 ounces each) classic white cake mix,** *Duncan Hines Moist Deluxe*®
4 **cups water**
9 **egg whites**
¼ **cup plus 2 tablespoons vegetable oil**
1 **jar (16-ounce) seedless red raspberry jam**
1 **container (16-ounce) vanilla frosting,** *Betty Crocker Rich & Creamy*®
3 **boxes (24 ounces each) ready-to-use pure white rolled fondant,** *Wilton*®
Powdered sugar, for dusting work surface

Special Equipment and Decorations
3 **round cake pans with 3-inch sides (one 10-inch, one 7-inch, and one 5-inch)**
3 **cardboard cake rounds (one 10-inch, one 7-inch, and one 5-inch)**
Silver dragées
4 **12⅜-inch (⅜-inch diameter) plastic dowel rods,** *Wilton*®
Small rhinestone crown or tiara, available at beauty supply stores (optional)

1. Preheat oven to 350 degrees F. Butter and flour cake pans. Combine 2 of the cake mixes, 2⅔ cups water, 6 egg whites, and ¼ cup oil in large bowl. Beat for 3 minutes or until well blended. Transfer all but 1 cup of batter to prepared 10-inch pan. Spoon reserved 1 cup of batter into prepared 7-inch pan. Combine remaining cake mix, 1⅓ cups water, 3 egg whites, and 2 tablespoons oil in empty large bowl used above. Beat for 2 minutes or until well blended. Spoon 2 cups of batter into prepared 5-inch pan; spoon remaining batter into partially filled 7-inch pan.

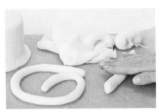

2. Bake 10-inch cake for 1½ hours, 7-inch cake for 55 minutes, and 5-inch cake for 35 minutes or until toothpick inserted into centers of cakes comes out clean. Cool in pans on cooling racks for 20 minutes. Invert cakes onto cooling racks, remove pans, and cool completely.

3. For filling, cut cakes horizontally in half. Spoon 1 tablespoon of jam into center of each cardboard round. Place 10-inch cake top, cut side up, on 10-inch cardboard; spread with ¾ cup of jam. Top with 10-inch cake bottom, cut side down. Repeat with remaining cakes and cardboard rounds, spreading ⅓ cup of jam between 7-inch cake layers and 3 tablespoons of jam between 5-inch cake layers. Spread frosting over cakes. Refrigerate for about 1 hour.

4. To decorate, sprinkle work surface and rolling pin with powdered sugar. Knead contents of 1 box of fondant until soft. Roll out fondant into 16-inch round that is ¼ inch thick, rotating to prevent sticking. Pierce bubbles that appear in fondant. Slide hands under fondant and drape over 10-inch cake; smooth over surface. Trim excess fondant from around base of cake. Brush off excess powdered sugar. Knead contents of second box of fondant until soft. Divide fondant in half, making 1 piece slightly larger. Follow above instructions to cover remaining cakes, rolling out larger fondant piece into 14-inch round for 7-inch cake and smaller fondant piece into 13-inch round for 5-inch cake. Roll remaining fondant into 3 ropes long enough to fit around cakes.

5. To assemble, cut dowel rods into nine 3-inch pieces. Place 10-inch cake on platter; press 4 cut rods into cake, positioning 3½ inches in from edge and spacing evenly. Press 1 rod into center. Next, press 3 cut rods into 7-inch cake, positioning 3 inches in from edge and spacing evenly. Press 1 cut rod into center. Place 7-inch cake on cardboard on top of rods in 10-inch cake. Place 5-inch cake on cake round on top of rods in 7-inch cake. Drape ropes around cake bases; decorate with silver dragées. Place crown on top of cake.

Baby Short Stacks

makes 12 **prep time** 10 minutes
baking time 30 minutes **cooling time** 45 minutes
decorating time 20 minutes

These little bundles of joy are the cutest things ever. Frost and decorate them in your shower colors, and these precious baby cakes will double as both decoration and dessert. They also make terrific take-home treats for the Mommy-to-be and guests alike.

Cake
1   **box (18.25-ounce) dark chocolate fudge cake mix,**
      Duncan Hines Moist Deluxe®
1   **cup water**
4   **eggs**
1   **box (3.9-ounce) chocolate instant pudding and pie filling mix,** *Jell-O®*
1/3   **cup vegetable oil**

Frosting
     Food coloring (color optional)
2   **containers (16 ounces each) classic vanilla frosting,**
      Duncan Hines Creamy Home-Style®

Special Decorations
4   **ounces pastel round quins (candy confetti) or multicolored sprinkles**

Cake
1. Preheat oven to 350 degrees F. Butter and flour a 13×9-inch baking pan.

2. Combine cake mix, water, eggs, pudding mix, and oil in large bowl. Beat for 2 minutes or until well blended. Pour batter into prepared pan.

3. Bake for 30 minutes or until toothpick inserted into center of cake comes out clean. Cool cake in pan on cooling rack for 15 minutes. Invert cake onto cooling rack, remove pan, and cool completely. Using a 2- or 3-inch round cookie cutter, cut cake into 12 pieces.

Frosting
4. Stir food coloring, 1 drop at a time, into frosting until desired color is achieved. Spread frosting over tops and sides of cakes to coat completely. Using toothpick, swirl frosting decoratively. Sprinkle cakes with quins.

Baby Fondant Packages

servings 30 to 40 **prep time** 15 minutes
baking time 1 ¼ hour
cooling time 1 hour **decorating time** 1 hour

Cake
- 3 boxes (18.25 ounces each) classic white cake mix, *Duncan Hines Moist Deluxe®*
- 4 cups water
- 9 egg whites
- ¼ cup plus 2 tablespoons vegetable oil
- 2 cups apricot preserves, *Smucker's®*

Fondant Decoration
- Powdered sugar, for dusting work surface
- 2 boxes (24 ounces each) ready-to-use pure white rolled fondant, *Wilton®*
- Green, red, blue, and yellow food coloring

Special Equipment and Decorations
- 1 10-inch square cake pan with 3-inch sides
- 1 8-inch square cake pan with 3-inch sides
- 2 square cardboard cake boards (one 10-inch and one 8-inch)
- 4 pairs disposable latex gloves
- Small moon- and star-shape cookie cutters
- Gum arabic
- Baby-theme decorations

Cake

1. Preheat oven to 350 degrees F. Butter and flour cake pans. Combine 2 of the cake mixes, 2⅔ cups water, 6 egg whites, and ¼ cup oil in large bowl. Beat for 3 minutes or until well blended. Pour batter into prepared 10-inch pan.

2. Combine remaining cake mix, 1⅓ cups water, 3 egg whites, and 2 tablespoons of oil in the emptied large bowl used in step 1. Beat for 2 minutes or until well blended. Pour batter into prepared 8-inch pan.

3. Bake 10-inch cake for 1 hour 15 minutes and 8-inch cake for 55 minutes or until toothpick inserted into centers of cakes comes out clean. Cool cakes in pans for 30 minutes. Invert cakes onto cooling racks and cool completely.

4. For glaze, stir preserves in heavy small saucepan over medium-high heat until beginning to boil. Strain preserves into small bowl. Spoon 1 tablespoon of glaze into center of each cardboard round. Place boards, glaze sides down, on top of cakes; invert. Brush remaining glaze over cakes.

Fondant Decoration

5. Sprinkle work surface and rolling pin with powdered sugar. Wearing latex gloves, knead green food coloring, 1 drop at a time, into fondant from 1 box. Roll out green fondant into 18-inch square that is ¼ inch thick, rotating to prevent sticking. Pierce any bubbles in fondant. Roll green fondant trimmings into rope long enough to fit around cake perimeter.

6. Slide hands under fondant and drape over 10-inch cake; smooth over surface. Trim excess fondant from around base of cake. Brush off excess powdered sugar. Place rope around cake.

7. Wearing second pair of latex gloves, measure out ½ cup fondant from second box; knead in red food coloring (just enough to make pink), 1 drop at a time. Measure out another ½ cup white fondant from the second box and wearing third pair of latex gloves, knead in blue food coloring, 1 drop at a time. Wrap pink and blue fondant pieces separately in plastic; set aside.

8. With the fourth pair of latex gloves, knead yellow food coloring, 1 drop at a time, into remaining fondant from second box. Roll out yellow fondant into 15-inch square that is ¼ inch thick. Slide hands under fondant and drape over 8-inch cake; smooth over surface. Trim excess fondant from base. Roll yellow fondant trimmings into rope long enough to fit around cake perimeter; place rope around cake. Place 8-inch cake on top of 10-inch cake.

9. Roll out pink and blue fondant separately into ¼-inch thickness. Cut shapes from fondant with cookie cutters. Moisten shapes with water, then dab gum arabic onto moistened side; press onto cakes to adhere. Top with baby-theme decorations.

Birthday
Stage Cake

servings 16 to 18 **prep time** 20 minutes
baking time 40 minutes **cooling time** 40 minutes
decorating time 30 minutes

2   boxes (18.25 ounces each) strawberry cake mix,
        Pillsbury Moist Supreme®
2²/₃ cups water
1   cup vegetable oil
6   eggs
³/₄ cup strawberry jam
2   containers (12 ounces each) fluffy white, lemon, or strawberry
        frosting, *Betty Crocker Whipped*®

Special Decoration
   Assorted circus-theme decorations

1. Preheat oven to 350 degrees F. Butter and flour two 9-inch round
cake pans with 2-inch sides.

2. Combine cake mixes, water, oil, and eggs in large bowl; beat for
3 minutes. Divide batter evenly between prepared pans.

3. Bake for 40 minutes or until toothpick inserted into centers of cakes
comes out clean. Cool cakes in pans on cooling rack for 15 minutes.
Invert cakes onto cooling rack, remove pans, and cool completely.

4. Cut 1 cake in half horizontally. Place top cake layer, cut side up, on
serving platter. Spread ¹/₂ cup of jam over cake layer. Top with bottom
cake layer, cut side down. Cut second cake vertically in half, forming
2 half-circle pieces. Spread remaining jam over top of 1 half-circle cake.
Top with second half-circle cake.

5. Place stacked half-circle cakes on top of cake on platter. Spread
entire cake with frosting to coat completely. Arrange circus-theme
decorations on cake to resemble circus stage.

Mocha Cake with Chocolate Crown

servings 12 to 16 **prep time** 30 minutes
baking time 35 minutes **cooling time** 45 minutes
chilling time 1½ hours **decorating time** 30 minutes

Cake

1⅓ cups hot water

½ cup instant coffee crystals, *Maxwell House®*

1 box (18.25-ounce) devil's food cake mix, *Duncan Hines Moist Deluxe®*

½ cup vegetable oil

3 eggs

Filling and Frosting

¼ cup instant coffee crystals, *Maxwell House®*

2 tablespoons hot water

1 container (8-ounce) frozen whipped topping, thawed, *Cool Whip®*

1 container (16-ounce) classic chocolate fudge frosting, *Duncan Hines Creamy Home-Style®*

Chocolate Crown

1 package (12-ounce) semisweet chocolate morsels, *Nestlé®*

1½ cups premier white morsels, *Nestlé®*
Additional semisweet chocolate morsels, *Nestlé®*

Cake

1. Preheat oven to 350 degrees F. Butter and flour two 8-inch round cake pans. Stir hot water and coffee crystals in large bowl until crystals dissolve. Add cake mix, oil, and eggs to coffee mixture. Beat for 2 minutes or until well blended.

2. Divide batter between prepared pans. Bake for 35 minutes or until toothpick inserted into centers of cakes comes out clean. Cool cakes in pans on cooling racks for 15 minutes. Invert cakes onto cooling racks and cool completely.

Filling and Frosting

3. Stir coffee crystals and hot water in medium bowl until crystals dissolve. Refrigerate for 30 minutes or until cold. Fold whipped topping into cold coffee mixture until just blended; set coffee cream aside.

4. Cut each cake horizontally in half. Place top cake layer, cut side up, on serving platter. Spread 1 cup of coffee cream on top of cake. Top with bottom cake layer, cut side down. Spread 1 cup of coffee cream over second cake layer. Repeat layering with third cake layer and remaining coffee cream. Top with remaining bottom cake layer, cut side down. Refrigerate for 30 minutes. Spread chocolate frosting evenly over cake to cover completely. Return to refrigerator.

Chocolate Crown

5. Draw three 6-inch-high crown designs over three 15-inch-long sheets of parchment paper. Cut out designs from parchment paper. Lay each crown template on large cookie sheet.

6. Melt 12 ounces chocolate morsels in microwave for 2½ minutes, or until melted and smooth, stirring every 30 seconds. Repeat with white morsels. Using offset spatula or pastry brush, spread melted chocolate thickly over 1 side of 2 of the crown templates. Repeat with melted white morsels and remaining crown template. Arrange additional chocolate morsels on white crown. Refrigerate for 30 minutes or until set.

7. Wrap 1 chocolate template, paper side out, around half of cake; carefully peel off paper. Wrap second chocolate crown, paper side out, around remaining half of cake; carefully peel off paper. Seal ends of crowns with hot knife. Refrigerate cake until chocolate crown is completely firm. Wrap white crown, paper side inward, around 5-inch-diameter bowl. Refrigerate until white crown is completely firm. Carefully peel paper from white crown. Place white crown on top of cake.

Strawberry
Tuxedo Cake

servings 10 to 12 **prep time** 10 minutes
baking time 20 minutes **cooling time** 45 minutes
chilling time 30 minutes **decorating time** 25 minutes

1   box (18.25-ounce) classic white cake mix, *Duncan Hines Moist Deluxe®*
1 1/3 cups water
3   eggs
2   tablespoons vegetable oil
3/4 cup strawberry jam
1   container (16-ounce) classic vanilla frosting, *Duncan Hines Creamy Home-Style®*
3/4 cup ready-to-use pure white rolled fondant, *Wilton®*
1/4 cup semisweet chocolate mini morsels, *Nestlé®*
10 to 12 tuxedo strawberries (see photos, below) or purchased
      chocolate-dipped strawberries

1. Preheat oven to 350 degrees F. Butter and flour four 8-inch round cake pans.

2. Combine cake mix, water, eggs, and oil in large bowl. Beat for 2 minutes or until well blended. Divide batter among prepared pans. Bake for 20 minutes or until toothpick inserted into centers of cakes comes out clean. Cool cakes in pans on cooling racks for 15 minutes.

3. Invert cakes onto cooling racks, remove pans, and cool completely. Spread 1/4 cup of jam over the top of each of 3 cakes. Place cake layers on top of each other on serving platter, ending with plain cake layer. Spread frosting smoothly over top and sides of cake to coat completely. Refrigerate for 30 minutes.

4. To decorate, roll out 1/4 cup of fondant into thin 10-inch-long log. Cut log crosswise into small pieces and roll into pea-size balls. Gently flatten each ball into button shape. Roll out remaining 1/2 cup of fondant between 2 sheets of plastic wrap to 1/8-inch thickness. Cut out 1-inch squares. Cut each square diagonally in half to form triangles. Remove cake from refrigerator. Using fork, draw lines through chilled frosting to resemble pleats.

5. Gently press fondant triangles into frosting around top edge of cake to resemble bow ties. Gently press fondant buttons below bow ties into frosting. Press a chocolate mini morsel into center of each bow tie. Garnish with tuxedo strawberries or chocolate-dipped strawberries.

Variation: To make 3 to 4 smaller cakes for single servings, divide the batter into 3 to 4 equal portions and bake in 3-inch miniature cake pans. Frost and decorate as instructed and serve on individual cake pedestals or dessert plates.

The Perfect Package

servings 30 to 35 **prep time** 35 minutes
baking time 30 minutes **cooling time** 45 minutes
decorating time 25 minutes

Cake
3   boxes (18.25 ounces each) classic white cake mix,
      Duncan Hines Moist Deluxe®
4   cups water
9   egg whites
¼   cup plus 2 tablespoons vegetable oil

Filling and Glaze
1   package (8-ounce) cream cheese, at room temperature,
      Philadelphia®
1   stick (4-ounce) butter, at room temperature
2   tablespoons almond-flavor liqueur, *Amaretto di Saronno®*
3½ cups powdered sugar
1   jar (16-ounce) apricot preserves, *Smucker's®*
1   tablespoon water

Fondant Decoration
2   boxes (24 ounces each) ready-to-use pure white rolled
      fondant, *Wilton®*
    Blue food coloring
    Powdered sugar, for dusting work surface

Special Equipment and Decorations
3   9-inch square baking pans with 2½-inch sides
    Disposable latex gloves
    Gum arabic
    White ribbon (1 inch wide)

Cake
1. Preheat oven to 350 degrees F. Butter and flour three
9-inch square cake pans. Combine cake mixes, water, egg
whites, and oil in very large bowl. Beat for 3 minutes or until
well blended. Divide batter evenly among prepared pans.

2. Bake for 30 minutes or until toothpick inserted into centers
of cakes comes out clean. Cool cakes in pans on cooling racks
for 15 minutes. Invert cakes onto racks and cool completely.

Filling and Glaze
3. Beat cream cheese, butter, and almond-flavor liqueur in
large bowl until smooth. Gradually beat in powdered sugar.

4. Place 1 cake layer on serving platter. Spread half of filling
over top of cake. Top with second cake layer. Spread
remaining filling over top of cake; top with third cake layer.
Trim any uneven sides or edges to make perfect square-
shaped box.

5. Stir preserves and water in small saucepan over high heat
until beginning to boil. Strain preserves into small bowl. Brush
glaze over cake to coat completely. Refrigerate cake.

Fondant Decoration
6. Wearing gloves, knead food coloring, 1 drop at a time, into
fondant until desired color is achieved. Wrap one-fourth of
blue fondant in plastic; set aside. Sprinkle work surface and
rolling pin with powdered sugar. Flatten remaining fondant
into square. Roll out fondant square into 26-inch square that
is ¼ inch thick, rotating to prevent sticking. Pierce bubbles that
appear in fondant. Slide hands under fondant and drape over
cake; smooth over surface. Trim excess fondant from around
base of cake. Brush off excess powdered sugar.

7. Form reserved one-fourth of blue fondant into long rope.
With a rolling pin, flatten fondant rope into band 25 inches
long and 2½ inches wide. Trim band to 2-inch width. Using
gum arabic as glue, wrap fondant band around top edge of
cake to resemble box lid. Wrap ribbon around cake to
resemble gift. Tie remaining ribbon into bow; place on top
of cake.

  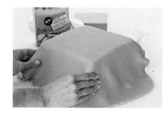 

Life's a Beach Cake

servings 8 prep time 15 minutes

1 purchased (10- to 12-ounce) angel food cake
10 large marshmallows, *Kraft Jet-Puffed*®
2 containers (16 ounces each) vanilla frosting,
　　Betty Crocker Rich & Creamy®
　　Blue food coloring
1/2 cup sweetened flaked coconut, *Baker's*®

Special Equipment and Decorations
　　Pastry bag
　　Large star tip
3 **paper wooden skewer umbrellas**
　　Jellied octopus candy and chocolate seashell candy

1. Place cake, wide end down, on serving platter. Fill hole in center of cake with marshmallows.

2. Spread contents of 1½ containers of frosting evenly over top and sides of cake to coat completely. Stir blue food coloring, 1 drop at a time, into remaining frosting until desired color is achieved. Transfer blue frosting to pastry bag fitted with star tip. Pipe frosting around base of cake.

3. Starting at base of cake and swirling in semicircular upward motion, drag wooden skewer through blue-colored frosting to form wave design. Arrange umbrellas on top of cake. Arrange jellied candy octopus and chocolate seashells on cake. Sprinkle coconut around base of cake.

Tropical Banana Cake

servings 14 prep time 15 minutes

2 purchased (10 to 12 ounces each) angel food cakes
2 containers (16 ounces each) vanilla frosting,
　　Betty Crocker Rich & Creamy®
1 teaspoon imitation banana extract, *McCormick*®
　　Yellow food coloring
1 ripe banana, mashed
2 cups sweetened flaked coconut, *Baker's*®
1 cup fruit-shape candies

Special Decoration
1 **palm tree decoration**

1. Place 1 cake, wide end down, on platter. Stir frosting and banana extract in large bowl to blend. Stir in yellow food coloring, 1 drop at a time, until desired color is achieved. Transfer ½ cup of banana frosting to small bowl and stir in mashed banana; spread over cake.

2. Cut one 2-inch-wide wedge from second cake; set aside. Spread ¼ cup of banana frosting over cut ends of second cake. Bring cut ends of second cake together, pressing to attach.

3. Place second cake, wide end down, on top of cake on platter. Tear reserved cake wedge into cubes. Fill hole in center of cakes with cake cubes. Spread remaining banana frosting evenly over top and sides of cake to coat completely. Sprinkle cake with coconut, pressing lightly to attach. Place palm tree decoration on top of cake. Arrange fruit-shape candies around palm tree and base of cake.

Holidays
The Recipes

Raspberry Fondue with Meringue Cloud Hearts

makes 2½ cups fondue and 20 meringue cookies
fondue prep time 15 minutes **meringue prep time** 15 minutes
baking time 1 hour **cooling time** 20 minutes

Meringue Cloud Hearts
2   **egg whites, at room temperature**
⅛   **teaspoon cream of tartar, *McCormick*®**
        Pinch of salt
½   **cup granulated sugar**
        Food coloring (optional)

Fondue
¾   **cup heavy cream**
1   **bag (12-ounce) premier white morsels, *Nestlé*®**
⅔   **cup seedless red raspberry jam**
¼   **cup white chocolate liqueur, *Godiva*®**

Special Equipment
        Pastry bag
        #2 star tip

Meringue Cloud Hearts
1. Preheat oven to 200 degrees F. Line 2 heavy large cookie sheets with parchment paper. Place egg whites in clean large metal bowl. Beat on medium speed until foamy. Add cream of tartar and increase speed to high. Continue beating until soft peaks form; mix in salt. Gradually add sugar, 1 tablespoon at a time, beating until stiff peaks form, about 5 minutes. If desired, add food coloring, 1 drop at a time, until desired color is achieved.

2. Transfer meringue mixture to pastry bag fitted with star tip. Pipe 2-inch heart-shape meringues onto prepared cookie sheets, spacing evenly apart. Bake for 1 hour or until dry and crispy when broken in half. Cool meringues completely on baking sheets. Store in airtight container at room temperature.

Fondue
3. Heat cream in medium saucepan over medium heat until bubbles appear; remove from heat. Add white morsels and whisk until melted and smooth. Stir in raspberry jam, then chocolate liqueur. Transfer mixture to fondue pot. To keep fondue warm at the table for an extended period, place over candle or canned-heat burner. To serve and eat immediately, spoon into a decorative gravy boat. Serve fondue with Meringue Cloud Hearts for dipping.

Dipping Variations: Use cubes of pound cake, fresh strawberries, marshmallows, or dried fruit.

Strawberry Cake with Real Strawberry Frosting

servings 8 to 10 **prep time** 10 minutes
baking time 25 minutes **cooling time** 45 minutes
decorating time 10 minutes **chilling time** 40 minutes

This cake-on-a-cake confection is poetry on a plate. Topped with a seductive swirl of strawberry frosting and fresh berries, this dessert spells sweet romance any way you slice it.

Cake
- 1 box (18.25-ounce) strawberry cake mix, *Betty Crocker SuperMoist*®
- 1 can (11.5-ounce) strawberry nectar, *Kerns*®
- 3 eggs
- ¼ cup vegetable oil

Filling and Frosting
- 2 containers (16 ounces each) strawberry frosting, *Betty Crocker Rich & Creamy*®
- 1 pound fresh strawberries, cleaned

Cake
1. Preheat oven to 350 degrees F. Butter and flour two 9-inch round cake pans. Combine cake mix, nectar, eggs, and oil in large bowl. Beat for 2 minutes or until well blended. Divide batter evenly between prepared pans.

2. Bake for 25 minutes or until toothpick inserted into centers of cakes comes out clean. Cool cakes in pans on cooling racks for 15 minutes. Invert cakes onto cooling rack and cool completely.

Filling and Frosting
3. Slice enough strawberries to make ³/₄ cup. Using serrated knife, cut each cake horizontally in half, forming 4 layers. Place 1 cake layer, cut side down, on serving platter.

4. Spread ¹/₃ cup of frosting over top of cake layer. Arrange ¹/₄ cup of sliced strawberries in single layer on top of frosting. Top with second cake layer, cut side down. Repeat layering with frosting and sliced strawberries. Top with third cake layer, cut side down. Repeat layering with frosting and remaining sliced strawberries. Top with remaining cake layer, cut side down.

5. Spread remaining frosting evenly over top and sides of cake to coat completely. Slice enough remaining whole strawberries to cover top of cake. Arrange sliced strawberries and 1 whole strawberry decoratively on top of cake. Refrigerate cake for 40 minutes. Serve cake with remaining whole strawberries.

Chocolate-Covered Cherries

makes 40 cherries **prep time** 20 minutes
chilling time 40 minutes

These chocolate-covered cherries are absolutely addictive. For a fun yet elegant dessert, pour a splash of cherry syrup into a martini glass, then top off with white- and dark-dipped cherries. For a more spirited dessert, spike the syrup with brandy or a fruit liqueur, like Grand Marnier®. Eat the cherries, then drink the syrup for a nightcap chaser. To add black-tie style to a dinner party or buffet, group filled glasses on stacked silver trays and have them do double duty as a centerpiece, or set a filled glass at each place setting to complete your tablescape. To make thoughtful gifts for anniversaries and other special days, fill a red take-out container and give that special someone a box of cherry bonbons.

40 maraschino cherries with stems (packed in heavy syrup), drained well
$^1/_2$ cup (3 ounces) semisweet chocolate morsels, *Nestlé*®
$^1/_2$ cup (3 ounces) premier white morsels, *Nestlé*®

1. Line cookie sheet with parchment paper or waxed paper. Pat cherries dry with paper towels.

2. Melt semisweet chocolate and white morsels separately in stainless-steel bowls set over pans of simmering water, stirring until smooth.

3. Holding stem of cherry, dip cherry into either melted chocolate or melted white morsels to coat. Transfer dipped cherry to prepared cookie sheet. Repeat with remaining cherries and melted chocolate or melted white morsels. Refrigerate for about 40 minutes or until set.

Chocolate Truffles

makes 36 truffles **prep time** 15 minutes
chilling time 1 hour

In France, chocolate truffles are more than dessert; they're a national pastime. It's easy to see why, especially when the truffles are as sinfully chocolaty as these. Don't worry about shaping them into precise balls—it's the little peaks that give them charm. Truffles freeze beautifully, so make several batches and store them in the freezer for impromptu gifts, drop-by guests, or spur-of-the-moment gatherings. To celebrate holidays or birthdays with sweet style, mix truffles with cookies or candy on a dessert tray or in a gift box. You'll make someone—or lots of someones—happy.

- 1 container (16-ounce) chocolate frosting, *Betty Crocker Rich & Creamy*®
- ¾ cup powdered sugar, sifted
- 1 teaspoon pure vanilla extract, *McCormick*®
- ½ cup unsweetened cocoa powder, *Hershey's*®

1. Line 2 cookie sheets with parchment paper. Beat frosting, powdered sugar, and vanilla in large bowl until smooth.

2. Using tablespoon or 1-ounce cookie scoop, form mixture into balls and place on prepared cookie sheet.

3. Dust truffles with cocoa powder. Cover and refrigerate truffles at least 1 hour before serving.

Truffle variations:
Instead of dusting the truffles with cocoa powder, chill them until slightly firm, then dip them in chocolate sprinkles, chopped nuts, toasted coconut, or semisweet chocolate mini morsels.

Instead of dusting the truffles with cocoa powder, chill them until slightly firm, then dip them in melted semisweet chocolate or white chocolate, then roll them in chopped nuts.

Substitute the vanilla extract with orange, peppermint, almond, or rum extract.

Form the truffle mixture around the following before dusting, rolling, or dipping: unwrapped Hershey's Kisses® or Hershey's Kisses with Almonds®, small Reese's Peanut Butter Cups®, or well-drained maraschino cherries.

Easter Bunny Cake

servings 8 to 10 **prep time** 30 minutes
baking time 45 minutes **cooling time** 45 minutes
decorating time 20 minutes

Cake and Frosting

1   box (18.25-ounce) classic yellow cake mix, *Duncan Hines Moist Deluxe*®
1¹⁄₃ cups water
¹⁄₃   cup vegetable oil
3   eggs
2   containers (16 ounces each) strawberry frosting,
     Betty Crocker Rich & Creamy®
1   bag (14-ounce) sweetened flaked coconut, *Baker's*®

Decorations

¹⁄₂   cup milk chocolate morsels, melted, *Nestlé*®
1   big chocolate chunk cookie, cut in half, *Pepperidge Farm*®
2   semisweet chocolate morsels, *Nestlé*®
1   sugar-coated gumdrop candy
1   red licorice lace, cut into 6 equal pieces
2   miniature marshmallows, *Kraft Jet-Puffed*®
3   large marshmallows, *Kraft Jet-Puffed*®

Special Equipment

1   6-inch metal bowl (ovenproof)
1   8-inch metal bowl (ovenproof)
    Wooden toothpicks

Cake and Frosting

1. Preheat oven to 350 degrees F. Butter and flour the 2 metal bowls. Combine cake mix, water, oil, and eggs in clean large mixing bowl. Beat for 2 minutes or until well blended. Pour 2 cups of batter into prepared 6-inch bowl; pour remaining batter into prepared 8-inch bowl.

2. Bake smaller cake for 40 minutes and larger cake for 45 minutes or until toothpick inserted into centers of cakes comes out clean. Cool cakes in bowls on cooling rack for 30 minutes. Invert cakes onto cooling rack, remove bowls, and cool completely.

3. Cut larger cake in half, forming 2 half-moon pieces. Spread ¹⁄₄ cup of frosting over flat top of each piece. Place pieces, cut sides down, on work surface, placing frosted sides together. Trim 1 inch from 1 end of cake; discard trimmings. Repeat entire process with smaller cake. Place larger cake on serving platter. Spread 2 tablespoons of frosting over trimmed end of smaller cake. Place trimmed end of smaller cake against trimmed end of larger cake. Spread remaining frosting over cakes to cover completely. Sprinkle with all but ¹⁄₂ cup of coconut, pressing so that it adheres.

Decorations

4. Brush melted milk chocolate over both sides of cookie halves to coat completely. Sprinkle with reserved ¹⁄₂ cup of coconut; set aside until dry.

5. Press 2 semisweet chocolate morsels onto bunny face for eyes. Using toothpicks for all, secure gumdrop candy onto bunny face for nose; licorice pieces onto bunny face for whiskers; and miniature marshmallows onto bunny face for teeth. Make 2-inch-deep cuts on top of bunny head; insert cookie halves for ears. Roll large marshmallows together; using toothpick, secure onto bunny for tail.

Mom's Strawberry Shortcake

servings 6 to 8 **prep time** 10 minutes **baking time** 10 minutes
cooling time 40 minutes **assembly time** 10 minutes

4²/₃ **cups all-purpose baking mix,** *Bisquick*®
1   **cup whole milk**
¹/₄ **cup plus 1 tablespoon butter, melted**
¹/₄ **cup plus 1 tablespoon granulated sugar**
2   **pounds fresh strawberries, sliced**
1   **container (16-ounce) frozen whipped topping, thawed,**
      ***Cool Whip*®**
     Additional whole fresh strawberries

Special Ingredients
  Rose petals* **(optional)**

1. Preheat oven to 425 degrees F. Butter two 8-inch round baking pans. Combine baking mix, milk, ¹/₄ cup of butter, and ¹/₄ cup of sugar in large bowl. Mix just until soft dough forms.

2. Press dough into prepared pans, dividing equally. Brush tops of dough with remaining 1 tablespoon of butter; sprinkle with remaining 1 tablespoon of sugar. Bake for 10 minutes or until golden brown.

3. Cool shortcakes in pans on cooling racks for 15 minutes. Invert shortcakes onto cooling racks, remove pans, and cool completely. Using potato masher, coarsely mash half of sliced strawberries in large bowl. Fold whipped topping into mashed berries; set berry cream aside.

4. To assemble, using serrated knife, cut shortcakes horizontally in half. Reserve most attractive shortcake layer top. Place 1 shortcake layer, cut side up, on serving platter. Top with one-third of berry cream, then with one-third of remaining sliced strawberries. Repeat layering 2 times. Top with reserved shortcake layer. Decorate with rose petals and whole strawberries (remove petals before cutting and serving). Serve immediately.

*****Note:** If using rose petals, purchase them from organic growers or cut them from chemical-free gardens. Avoid using florists' flowers, since they are often sprayed with chemicals that could rub off on food. Never consume a flower unless it is known to be edible.

Fourth of July
Angel Food Cake

servings 14 prep time 15 minutes

2 purchased (10 to 12 ounces each) angel food cakes
2½ containers (16 ounces each) vanilla frosting,
      Betty Crocker Rich & Creamy®
1 box (4.5-ounce) strawberry-flavored fruit snacks,
      Betty Crocker Fruit by the Foot®
1 pint fresh blueberries

Special Equipment
   Pastry bag
   Large star tip

1. Place 1 cake, wide end down, on serving platter. Spread thin layer of frosting over top of cake.

2. Cut one 2-inch-wide wedge from second cake. Spread ¼ cup of frosting over cut ends of second cake. Bring cut ends of second cake together, pressing to attach.

3. Place second cake on top of cake on platter. Tear cake wedge into cubes. Fill hole in center of cakes with cake cubes. Spread 1 whole container of frosting evenly over top and sides of cake to coat completely.

4. Cut fruit roll strips to match height of cake. Press fruit roll strips vertically onto sides of cake to resemble stripes, spacing evenly. Arrange blueberries decoratively on top of cake.

5. Transfer remaining frosting to pastry bag fitted with star tip. Pipe frosting decoratively around upper and lower edges of cake. Pipe stars on top of blueberries.

Apple Crisp Pie

servings 6 prep time 10 minutes chilling time 10 minutes

1½ cups cold whole milk
1 box (3.4-ounce) vanilla instant pudding and pie
      filling mix, *Jell-O®*
1½ teaspoons ground cinnamon, *McCormick®*
1 (6-ounce) premade graham cracker piecrust,
      Keebler Ready Crust®
1 container (21-ounce) sliced apple pie filling or topping,
      Comstock More Fruit®
2 (1.5 ounces each) crunchy granola bars, *Nature Valley®*

1. Combine milk, pudding mix, and 1 teaspoon of the cinnamon in large bowl. Beat for 2 minutes or until well blended and beginning to thicken. Pour into graham cracker piecrust. Refrigerate for 10 minutes.

2. Stir apple pie filling with remaining ½ teaspoon of cinnamon in medium bowl to blend; spread over pudding. Cover pie; refrigerate until ready to serve.

3. Enclose granola bars in resealable plastic bag. Using a rolling pin, crush bars into coarse crumbs. Sprinkle pie with granola crumbs and serve.

Crunchy Doughnut Eyeballs

makes 20 treats prep time 30 minutes
chilling time 10 minutes

20 glazed doughnut holes, *Entenmann's®*
1 cup premier white morsels, *Nestlé®*
2 tablespoons solid vegetable shortening, *Crisco®*
20 *Life Savers Gummies®*
20 mini candy-coated milk chocolate candies, *M&M's Minis®*
2 drops red food coloring

1. Line cookie sheet with parchment paper or waxed paper. Cut ⅛-inch-thick slices from 2 opposite sides of each doughnut hole.

2. Melt white morsels and vegetable shortening in top of double boiler or in glass bowl in microwave.

3. Using fork, and working with 1 doughnut hole at a time, dip into melted morsels mixture to coat. Lift coated doughnut holes from coating, shaking excess melted morsels mixture back into bowl. Place coated doughnut holes, 1 cut side down, on prepared cookie sheet.

4. Place jellied candies on top of coated doughnuts. Dab chocolate candies with some of remaining melted morsels mixture and press onto jellied candies. Refrigerate for 10 minutes or until coating is set.

5. Stir 2 tablespoons of remaining melted morsels mixture and 2 drops of food coloring in small bowl to blend. Using toothpick, paint colored morsels mixture on doughnut eyeballs to resemble veins. Refrigerate until ready to serve.

Caramel Parfaits

makes 8 prep time 15 minutes
chilling time 2 hours

1 cup boiling water
1 box (3-ounce) instant orange gelatin dessert mix, *Jell-O®*
1 cup cold water
4 containers (3.5 ounces each) prepared butterscotch-flavored pudding, *Kraft Handi-Snacks®*
1 cup frozen whipped topping, thawed, *Cool Whip®*

Special Decorations
Assorted Halloween candies

1. Combine boiling water and gelatin mix in large bowl; stir until gelatin dissolves. Stir cold water into gelatin. Divide gelatin equally among 8 parfait or champagne glasses. Refrigerate for 2 hours or until gelatin is set.

2. Spoon butterscotch pudding on top of gelatin in glasses, dividing equally. Spoon 2 tablespoons of whipped topping over pudding in each glass. Decorate whipped topping with assorted Halloween candies.

Halloween Pumpkin Cake

servings 14 **prep time** 15 minutes

2   purchased (10 to 12 ounces each) angel food cakes
    Red and yellow food coloring
2   containers (16 ounces each) vanilla frosting,
        Betty Crocker Rich & Creamy®
16 chocolate sandwich cookies, *Oreo®*
14 large marshmallows, *Kraft Jet-Puffed®*
1   container (8-ounce) frozen whipped topping,
        thawed, *Cool Whip®*
1   small chocolate log candy, cut in half, *Tootsie Roll®*

Special Equipment
    6-inch bamboo skewer
    Pastry bag
    Large plain tip

1. Place 1 cake, narrow end down, on serving platter. Stir food coloring, 1 drop at a time, into frosting in large bowl until desired orange color is achieved. Spread thin layer of frosting over top of cake.

2. Place second cake, narrow end up, on top of first cake to form pumpkin shape. Spread remaining frosting evenly over top and sides of cakes to coat completely.

3. Break cookies apart; scrape off filling. Enclose cookies in resealable plastic bag. Using rolling pin, crush cookies into fine crumbs. Sprinkle chocolate cookie crumbs on top of cake and around base of cake.

4. Skewer marshmallows on top of each other on wooden skewer. Place marshmallow skewer in hole in center of cake.

5. Spoon whipped topping into pastry bag fitted with plain tip. Pipe whipped topping over marshmallow stack to resemble ghost. Cut one half of chocolate log candy into two smaller pieces and shape into scary shapes for eyes. Shape second half of chocolate log into scary shape for mouth. Place eyes and mouth on ghost.

Mini Pumpkin Spice Cakes with Orange Glaze

servings 8 prep time 20 minutes
baking time 20 minutes cooling time 30 minutes
chilling time 10 minutes decorating time 15 minutes

1   box (18.25-ounce) spice cake mix, *Betty Crocker SuperMoist*®
1¼ cups water
⅓ cup vegetable oil
3   eggs
⅔ cup heavy cream
1   bag (12-ounce) premier white morsels, *Nestlé*®
    Red and yellow food coloring
1   package (7-ounce) marzipan, *Odense*®
    Green food coloring

Special Equipment
1   8-cup mini Bundt cake pan
    Disposable latex gloves
    Leaf-shape cookie cutter

1. Preheat oven to 350 degrees F. Butter and flour 8-cup mini Bundt cake pan. Combine cake mix, water, oil, and eggs in large bowl. Beat for 2 minutes or until well blended. Divide batter equally among prepared cups of pan.

2. Bake for 20 minutes or until toothpick inserted near centers of cakes comes out clean. Cool cakes in pans on cooling racks for 15 minutes. Invert cakes onto cooling rack, remove pans, and cool completely. Set cooling rack on top of cookie sheet.

3. For Orange Glaze, heat cream in small saucepan over medium heat until bubbles appear; remove from heat. Add white morsels and stir until melted and smooth. Stir in red and yellow food coloring, 1 drop at a time, until desired orange color is achieved. Drizzle glaze over cakes. Refrigerate cakes for 10 minutes or until glaze is firm. Cover and reserve any remaining glaze.

4. For stems and leaves, place marzipan in medium bowl. Using latex gloves, knead green food coloring, 1 drop at a time, into marzipan until desired color is achieved. Divide marzipan into 2 equal pieces. Roll 1 marzipan piece into 12-inch log. Cut log crosswise into eight 1½-inch pieces; set aside to use as stems. Flatten remaining marzipan piece, then place between 2 sheets of plastic wrap. Using rolling pin, roll out marzipan to ¼-inch thickness. Using leaf-shape cookie cutter or small sharp knife, cut out 24 leaves. Decorate cakes with marzipan stems and leaves.

5. Rewarm reserved glaze. Serve cakes, passing glaze alongside.

Maple Syrup Pecan Pie

servings 8 **prep time** 10 minutes
baking time 50 minutes **cooling time** 15 minutes

1¼ cups maple-flavored pancake syrup,
    Log Cabin Original Syrup®
⅓ cup packed golden brown sugar
3   eggs
1   egg yolk
2   teaspoons all-purpose flour
1½ teaspoons pure vanilla extract, *McCormick*®
2   tablespoons butter, melted
1½ cups pecan halves
1   9-inch frozen unbaked deep-dish pie shell,
    Marie Callender's®

1. Preheat oven to 350 degrees F. Stir syrup, sugar, eggs, egg yolk, flour, and vanilla in large bowl to blend. Whisk in melted butter (syrup mixture will be very thin at this point). Stir in 1 cup of pecans.

2. Place frozen pie shell on heavy cookie sheet. Carefully pour maple syrup mixture into pie shell. Arrange remaining ½ cup of pecans on top of syrup mixture, pressing into syrup mixture to coat.

3. Place baking sheet in center of oven. Bake pie for 50 minutes or until edges are golden and filling is just set in center. Cool pie on cooling rack for 15 minutes. Cut pie into wedges and serve warm or at room temperature.

Sweet Potato Pie with Marshmallow Creme

servings 6 **prep time** 10 minutes
baking time 35 minutes **cooling time** 1 hour

1 (6-ounce) premade graham cracker piecrust,
    Keebler Ready Crust®
1 can (15-ounce) candied sweet potatoes in syrup,
    drained, *Princess*®, or pure pumpkin, *Libby's*®
1 can (14-ounce) sweetened condensed milk, *Carnation*®
3 eggs
2 teaspoons pumpkin pie spice, *McCormick*®
1 jar (7-ounce) marshmallow creme, *Kraft Jet-Puffed*®
12 whole pecans, toasted

Special Equipment
Kitchen torch (optional)

1. Preheat oven to 350 degrees F. Place crust on heavy cookie sheet. Blend sweet potatoes or pumpkin, condensed milk, eggs, and pumpkin pie spice in blender until smooth. Pour mixture into crust.

2. Bake for 35 minutes or until filling puffs around edges and center is just set. Transfer pie to cooling rack and cool to room temperature.

3. Just before serving, spread marshmallow creme over pie. If desired, use kitchen torch to quickly caramelize marshmallow creme. Garnish with toasted pecans. Serve pie immediately.

Star of David Angel Food Cake

servings 8
prep time 15 minutes

An inexpensive faux pearl choker and Star of David topper make this easy angel food cake the star attraction at your holiday table. Just remove the pearls before cutting the cake so nobody swallows one!

1   purchased (10- to 12-ounce) angel food cake
10   large marshmallows, *Kraft Jet-Puffed*®
     Blue food coloring
1   container (12-ounce) fluffy white frosting, *Betty Crocker Whipped*®

Special Equipment
3   wired pearl strands

1. Place cake, wide end down, on serving platter. Fill hole in center of cake with marshmallows.

2. Stir food coloring, 1 drop at a time, into frosting in large bowl until desired color is achieved. Spread frosting evenly over top and sides of cake to coat completely.

3. Bend 2 pearl strands into 2 Stars of David, leaving 2 inches of wire hanging down from bottom of each star.

4. Place 1 Star of David inside and perpendicular to second Star of David, creating 3-D effect. Stand Stars of David on top of cake. Drape another pearl strand around base of cake. Remove pearls before cutting and serving.

Variation: Place the Star of David on top of the cake along with 9 silver candles.

Buttery Honey Cake

servings 12 to 16 **prep time** 15 minutes
baking time 45 minutes **cooling time** 30 minutes

1   box (18.25-ounce) classic yellow cake mix,
      Duncan Hines Moist Deluxe®
1   cup water
$^1/_3$ cup honey, *Sue Bee®*
$^1/_3$ cup margarine, melted
$^1/_3$ cup poppy seeds, *McCormick®*
3   eggs
$^1/_2$ teaspoon pumpkin pie spice, *McCormick®*
$^1/_4$ cup honey, *Sue Bee®*
$^1/_3$ cup powdered sugar, sifted

Special Equipment
   10-inch round pan with 2-inch sides

1. Preheat oven to 350 degrees F. Butter and flour 10-inch round cake pan with 2-inch sides.

2. Combine cake mix, water, $^1/_3$ cup of honey, margarine, poppy seeds, eggs, and pumpkin pie spice in large bowl. Beat for 2 minutes or until well blended. Pour into prepared pan.

3. Bake for 45 minutes or until toothpick inserted into center of cake comes out clean. Cool cake in pan on cooling rack for 15 minutes. Invert cake onto cooling rack and cool completely.

4. Using wooden or metal skewer, poke about 20 small holes all over top of cake. Drizzle the $^1/_4$ cup of honey over cake, allowing honey to sink into holes. Just before serving, dust with powdered sugar.

Nutcracker Holiday Cake

servings 10 to 12 **prep time** 10 minutes
baking time 30 minutes **cooling time** 30 minutes

This whimsical cake looks like it was baked by the Sugar Plum Fairy, but you can whip it up at home in less time than it takes to drive to the bakery. It tastes like a giant gingerbread cookie, frosted with swirling snowflakes of cream cheese frosting and topped with small wooden nutcrackers and tiny wrapped gifts sure to capture the fancy of young and old. (Both the nutcracker and gift decorations are available at crafts supply stores.) This charming confection makes a delightful centerpiece dessert throughout the holidays, but it's especially magical on Christmas Eve, when you can tell the story of the Nutcracker Prince and send everyone to bed with sweet dreams.

2   boxes (14.5 ounces each) gingerbread cake and cookie mix, *Krusteaz®*
2   cups water
2   eggs
1½ containers (16 ounces each) cream cheese frosting,
     Betty Crocker Rich & Creamy®

Special Decorations
     Wrapped present decorations
     Small wooden nutcrackers
     Glittered star decoration

1. Preheat oven to 350 degrees F. Butter and flour two 8-inch round cake pans.

2. Combine cake mixes, water, and eggs in large bowl. Beat for 2 minutes or until well blended.

3. Divide batter between prepared pans. Bake for 30 minutes or until toothpick inserted into centers of cakes comes out clean. Cool cakes in pans on cooling rack for 15 minutes. Invert cakes onto cooling racks, remove pans, and cool completely.

4. Place 1 cake layer on platter; spread ½ cup of frosting over top of cake. Top with second cake layer, flat side up. Spread remaining frosting over top and sides of cake to coat completely. Decorate cake with wrapped presents, wooden nutcrackers, and star. Remove decorations before cutting and serving.

Classic Holiday Wreath Cake

servings 8 **prep time** 15 minutes

1 purchased (10- to 12-ounce) angel food cake
  Green food coloring
1 container (16-ounce) vanilla frosting,
    Betty Crocker Rich & Creamy®
2 cups sweetened flaked coconut, *Baker's®*
3 purchased sugar leaf decorations, *Dec-A-Cake®*,
    or green decorating gel, *Cake Mate®*
3 hard cinnamon-flavored candies, *Red Hots®*,
    or red decorating gel, *Cake Mate®*

1. Place cake, wide end down, on serving platter. Stir food coloring, 1 drop at a time, into frosting in large bowl until desired color is achieved. Spread frosting evenly over top and sides of cake to coat completely.

2. Press coconut into frosting to resemble snow. Arrange sugar leaves on top of cake or pipe green gel on top of cake to resemble holly leaves. Arrange cinnamon-flavored candies on top of cake or pipe red gel on top of cake to resemble holly berries.

Spicy Wreath Fruit Cake

servings 12 **prep time** 10 minutes
baking time 45 minutes **cooling time** 30 minutes

12 ounces mixed glacé fruit, chopped
¹/₂ cup chopped walnuts, toasted
¹/₃ cup chopped pitted dates, *Sunsweet®*
1 box (18.25-ounce) spice cake mix,
    Betty Crocker SuperMoist®
1¹/₄ cups water
¹/₃ cup vegetable oil
3 eggs
2 teaspoons pure orange extract, *McCormick®*
2 teaspoons brandy extract, *McCormick®*
  Frozen whipped topping, thawed, *Cool Whip®* (optional)

1. Preheat oven to 350 degrees F. Butter and flour a 10-inch ring mold. Combine glacé fruit, walnuts, dates, and 3 tablespoons of dry cake mix in medium bowl; toss to coat.

2. Combine remaining cake mix, water, oil, and eggs in large bowl. Beat for 2 minutes or until well blended. Stir in orange and brandy extracts. Stir fruit and nut mixture into batter.

3. Transfer batter to prepared mold. Bake for 45 minutes or until toothpick inserted near center of cake comes out clean. Cool cake in pan on cooling rack for 15 minutes. Invert cake onto cooling rack, remove pan, and cool completely. Serve with a dollop of whipped topping (optional).

White Chocolate Yule Log with Snow Frosting

makes 2 yule logs (8 to 10 slices each)
prep time 15 minutes **baking time** 15 minutes
cooling time 20 minutes **freezing time** 30 minutes
decorating time 10 minutes

Cake
1   box (18.25-ounce) Swiss chocolate cake mix,
        Duncan Hines Moist Deluxe®
1¼ cups water
½   cup vegetable oil
3   eggs
¼   cup powdered sugar

Filling and Frosting
1   container (16-ounce) frozen whipped topping, thawed, *Cool Whip*®
1   container (12-ounce) fluffy white frosting, *Betty Crocker Whipped*®

Forest Mushrooms
10 large chocolate morsels, unwrapped, *Hershey's*® *Kisses*
10 miniature marshmallows, *Kraft Jet-Puffed*®
¼   cup powdered sugar

Cake
1. Position 1 rack in upper third of oven and second rack in center of oven; preheat to 350 degrees F. Line two 13×9×¾-inch baking pans with parchment paper, allowing 1 inch of paper to hang over sides.

2. Combine cake mix, water, oil, and eggs in large bowl. Beat for 2 minutes or until well blended. Divide batter between prepared pans; spread to cover pans evenly.

3. Bake for 15 minutes or until toothpick inserted into centers of cakes comes out clean, rotating pans halfway through baking. Sift powdered sugar over hot cakes. Working with 1 hot cake at a time, place clean kitchen towel on top of cake. Place large cutting board (larger than baking sheet) on top of towel on cake. Invert cake onto towel and cutting board. Remove pan and carefully peel off parchment paper. Starting at 1 long side and using towel as aid, gently roll up cake jelly-roll style (cake will crack). Repeat with second cake. Cool rolled cakes completely.

Filling and Frosting
4. Unroll cakes. Spread whipped topping evenly over cakes. Roll up cakes (without the towel) jelly-roll style, enclosing filling. Arrange cakes, seam sides down, on freezer-safe serving platters. Freeze cakes for 30 minutes or until firm (this will make them easier to frost). Spread white frosting over cakes to coat completely. Draw fork along length of cakes to form bark design. Refrigerate cakes.

Forest Mushrooms
5. Using small sharp knife, round tips of large chocolate morsels slightly to resemble mushroom caps. Insert 1 toothpick through each marshmallow, then into flat side of chocolate mushroom cap; place on cakes. Dust with powdered sugar.

Harvest Walnut Cookies

makes 6 dozen cookies **prep time** 20 minutes
baking time 10 minutes per batch

Vanilla Dough
1   **box (18.25-ounce) white cake mix, _Betty Crocker SuperMoist®_**
1/3 **cup vegetable oil**
4   **tablespoons butter, melted**
1   **egg, beaten**
1   **teaspoon pure vanilla extract, _McCormick®_**
3/4 **cup chopped walnuts, lightly toasted**

Chocolate Dough
1   **box (18.25-ounce) devil's food cake mix, _Betty Crocker SuperMoist®_**
1/3 **cup vegetable oil**
4   **tablespoons butter, melted**
1   **egg, beaten**
2   **teaspoons pure vanilla extract, _McCormick®_**
3/4 **cup chopped walnuts, lightly toasted**

Vanilla Dough
1. Beat cake mix, oil, melted butter, egg, and vanilla in large bowl until dough forms. Stir in walnuts.

Chocolate Dough
2. Beat cake mix, oil, melted butter, egg, and vanilla in large bowl until dough forms. Stir in walnuts.

Cookies
3. Preheat oven to 400 degrees F. Scoop 1 teaspoon of vanilla dough into ball. Scoop 1 teaspoon of chocolate dough into ball. Gently press dough balls together, then roll gently to form one ball. Continue, making 20 balls.

4. Place dough balls on heavy large ungreased cookie sheet, spacing evenly apart. Bake for 10 minutes, or just until cookies begin to brown. Cool cookies on cookie sheets for 5 minutes. Transfer cookies to wire racks and cool completely.

5. Repeat with remaining chocolate and vanilla dough, forming about 6 dozen cookies total. Store in airtight container at room temperature for up to 2 days or freeze for up to 3 months.

Sweet Blessings Apple Cake

servings 8 to 10 **prep time** 20 minutes
baking time 40 minutes **cooling time** 10 minutes

1 box (15-ounce) honey cornbread & muffin mix, *Krusteaz®*
1 cup whole milk
2 eggs
2 tablespoons yellow cornmeal, *Albers®*
1 container (21-ounce) apple pie filling or topping,
    Comstock More Fruit®
1½ cups low-fat granola, *Kellogg's®*
¾ cup honey, warmed, *Sue Bee®*

1. Preheat oven to 400 degrees F. Butter a 9-inch square or round baking pan.

2. Combine cornbread mix, milk, eggs, and cornmeal in large bowl. Stir until just moistened; stir in apple pie filling.

3. Transfer batter to prepared pan. Sprinkle granola over batter. Set aside for 15 minutes. Bake for 40 minutes or until toothpick inserted into center of cake comes out clean.

4. Cool cake for 10 minutes. Drizzle honey over warm cake and serve.

Kwanza Celebration Cake

servings 8 **prep time** 15 minutes

1 purchased (10- to 12-ounce) angel food cake
1 container (16-ounce) vanilla frosting,
    Betty Crocker Rich & Creamy®
2 tablespoons unsweetened cocoa powder, *Hershey's®*
2 teaspoons pure vanilla extract, *McCormick®*
1 teaspoon ground cinnamon, *McCormick®*
1 container (21-ounce) apple pie filling or topping,
    Comstock More Fruit®
1 package (1.7-ounce) *CornNuts®*
½ cup toasted pumpkin seeds
½ cup popped popcorn, *Orville Redenbacher's®*

Special Equipment
Kwanza candles

1. Using serrated knife, cut cake horizontally into 2 layers. Place bottom cake layer, cut side up, on serving platter.

2. Mix frosting, cocoa powder, vanilla, and cinnamon in large bowl to blend. Spread some frosting over top of cake layer on platter. Top with second cake layer, cut side down. Spread remaining frosting evenly over top and sides of cake to coat.

3. Spoon apple pie filling into hole in center of cake. Place candles on top of cake. Sprinkle top of cake with the popcorn and some of the CornNuts® and pumpkin seeds. Sprinkle remaining CornNuts® and pumpkin seeds around the base of cake.

Gift Goodies

No matter what kind of gift I take to a friend or a party, a gift of food is by far the most loved and appreciated. Buying something is thoughtful, but making it says, "I care enough to spend time on you." Of course, most of us don't have a lot of time to spend.

This chapter serves up food for thought, a wealth of ways to become the Giving Gourmet, sharing your sentiment without spending your life in the kitchen. Ice cream cones filled with candy make fabulous favors, while fun fondue served in a bow-tied jar and edible iced picture frames are personal ways to present a one-of-a-kind gift to a one-of-a-kind person. The best gift of all is the gift of you, so share freely, from your heart—and your kitchen.

The Recipes

Ice Cream Cone Favors

makes 12 cones **prep time** 25 minutes
chilling time 10 minutes

1   bag (12-ounce) premier white morsels, *Nestlé*
12 ice cream cones (flat-bottomed)
    Small chocolate candy toppings, nonpareils, and sprinkles

Special Equipment and ingredients
    Lollipops, sugar sticks, and other small packaged candies
12 4×9-inch cellophane bags
12 pieces ⁵⁄₈-inch sheer ribbon (each 10 inches long)

1. Line cookie sheet with waxed paper. In a small glass bowl, melt white morsels in microwave, stirring every 20 seconds until melted. Dip top and upper side tier of ice cream cone into melted white morsels; immediately roll coated areas of cone in small candy toppings to create decorative layer. Place cones on prepared cookie sheet and cool in refrigerator for 10 minutes or until candy has set.

2. Fill cone with lollipops and packaged candies. Slip filled cones into cellophane bags and tie with ribbon.

Poached Pears with Wine Sauce

servings 6 **prep time** 10 minutes
cooking time 30 minutes

1   cup port wine
¹⁄₂ cup granulated sugar
1   tablespoon ground cinnamon, *McCormick®*
1   tablespoon vanilla extract, *McCormick®*
1   lemon, sliced
1   orange, sliced
1   sprig rosemary (optional)
2   cans (15.25 ounces each) halved pears in syrup, *Del Monte®*
1   can (15-ounce) raspberry pie filling, *Oregon Fruit Products Co.®*
1   container (8-ounce) frozen whipped topping, thawed, *Cool Whip®*
     Fresh mint

1. In large saucepan, combine port wine, sugar, cinnamon, vanilla, lemon and orange slices, and rosemary (optional). Bring to a boil. Reduce heat and simmer for 10 minutes.

2. Add pears and syrup from cans. Add enough cold water to just cover pears. Return mixture to a simmer and then remove from heat, allowing pears to poach in liquid for 20 minutes (when pears are done, they will be tender and reddish in color). With a slotted spoon, remove lemon and orange slices from syrup and discard. Remove pears from syrup with slotted spoon and chill in refrigerator.

3. Add raspberry pie filling to syrup; bring to a boil over high heat. Reduce heat to medium and cook for 10 to 12 minutes, reducing syrup to a glaze (when glaze is ready it will coat the back of a spoon). Let cool to room temperature. To serve, spoon chilled pears into 6 bowls and top with glaze. Top with whipped topping and fresh mint.

Cookie Pots

makes 12 cookie pots **prep time** 25 minutes
chilling 1 hour 15 minutes **baking time** 10 minutes per batch
drying time 3 hours

2 **packages (18 ounces each) refrigerated sugar cookie dough,
   room temperature, *Pillsbury*®**
2 **teaspoons cherry extract, *McCormick*®**
1 **cup all-purpose flour**
   Flour, for dusting surface
   Tubes of colored decorating frosting

Special Equipment and ingredients
12 **8-inch lollipop sticks**
    3- to 4-inch flower-shape cookie cutters
12 **4-inch flower pots, decorated, if desired (tape hole in bottom of pot)**
    Crushed chocolate sandwich cookies, *Oreos*® (filling removed)

1. In large bowl, mix sugar cookie dough, cherry extract, and 1 cup flour with wooden spoon until flour is incorporated and firm dough forms. Divide in half, shape into disks, and wrap each disk in plastic wrap. Refrigerate for 1 hour.

2. Preheat oven to 350 degrees F. On lightly floured surface, roll 1 dough disk to ¼-inch thickness. Cut flower shapes with cookie cutters. (Be sure to cut cookies in multiples of two since they will be sandwiched together.) Place on ungreased cookie sheet and refrigerate for 15 minutes. Bake for 10 minutes or until edges are golden brown. Cool completely on cooling rack. Repeat with remaining disk of dough.

3. Decorate cookies with frosting; allow to harden, about 2 hours. Sandwich lollipop stick between 2 cookies using decorating frosting. Allow to dry for at least 1 hour. Place one cookie, lollipop stick end down, in a pot and fill the pot with crushed cookie crumbs. Repeat with remaining cookies, pots, and cookie crumbs.

Confectioner's
Frames

makes 6 frames **prep time** 25 minutes
freezing time 20 minutes **baking time** 10 minutes
frosting time 20 minutes

Refrigerated cookie dough is pretty as a picture when cookie-cuttered into shapes and decorated with colored frosting and snippets of candy. Attach a photo and wrap in clear cellophane bags for party favors, place cards, holiday ornaments, or treasured mementos for family and friends.

1   package (18-ounce) refrigerated sugar cookie dough,
      room temperature, *Pillsbury*®
1   teaspoon brandy extract, *McCormick*®
½   cup all-purpose flour
     Flour, for dusting work surface
     Assorted food coloring (optional)
1   container (16-ounce) white frosting, *Pillsbury*®
     Tubes of colored decorating frosting
     Assorted candies, for decoration

1. Preheat oven to 350 degrees F. In a bowl, knead cookie dough with brandy extract and flour to combine. On lightly floured surface, roll out dough to ¼-inch thickness.

2. Cut out 3-inch squares, rounds, or rectangles and place on ungreased cookie sheet. Cut out the center of each, leaving a space to fit a picture. Place cookie sheet in freezer for 20 minutes.

3. Bake for 10 minutes or until lightly browned around edges. Cool completely on cooling rack.

4. If desired, add food coloring to white frosting. Frost frames with white or colored frosting. Use tubes of colored decorating frosting to make designs. Decorate with assorted candies. Attach photo to the back of each frame with frosting.

Peach Fondue with Meringue Cookies

servings 6 **prep time** 10 minutes

A combination of creamy peach puree and rich white chocolate gives both fruit and chocolate lovers a gift they'll savor. For a sure-to-be-welcomed hostess or party gift, nestle a jar of fondue in a napkin-lined basket and accompany it with fluffy store-bought meringues or cubed pound cake for dipping.

$3/4$ **cup heavy cream**
1   **bag (12-ounce) premier white morsels,** *Nestlé*®
1   **can (15-ounce) peaches, drained and pureed,** *Dole*®
$1/4$ **cup white chocolate liqueur,** *Godiva*®
1   **package (5-ounce) meringue cookies**

1. In medium heavy saucepan, heat cream over medium heat until bubbles appear around edges; remove from heat.

2. Add white morsels and whisk until melted and smooth. Stir in peach puree; stir in white chocolate liqueur.

3. To keep fondue warm at the table for an extended period of time, transfer fondue to fondue pot. Place over candle or canned burner to keep warm. To serve and eat immediately, transfer fondue to decorative gravy boat. Serve fondue with meringue cookies or dipping variations.

Dipping variations: pound cake cubes, fresh strawberries, marshmallows, or dried fruit

Chocolate
Phyllo Fans

makes 12 fans **prep time** 25 minutes
baking time 10 minutes **chilling time** 10 minutes

24 plain phyllo pastry sheets, cut into 8×8-inch squares, *Athens*®
    Butter-flavored cooking spray, *PAM*®
1   package (7-ounce) semisweet dipping chocolate, *Baker's*®,
    or semisweet chocolate morsels, *Nestlé*®
¾ cup chopped almonds

1. Preheat oven to 375 degrees F. Line a cookie sheet with parchment paper; set aside.

2. Lay out one 8×8-inch square of phyllo and lightly spray with cooking spray. Place second square on top. Fold phyllo squares in half and lightly spray both sides with cooking spray. Fold phyllo accordion-style in ½-inch folds. Fan out long end that was originally folded over, keeping other end pinched together. Carefully place on prepared cookie sheet. Repeat until all phyllo squares are used.

3. Bake for 10 minutes or until fans are golden brown. Remove phyllo fans from oven and cool completely on a cooling rack.

4. In a small bowl, microwave chocolate 30 seconds at a time, stirring after each interval until chocolate is melted. Dip top of fan into chocolate; immediately dip into chopped almonds. Place phyllo fans back on cookie sheet and let set in refrigerator for 10 minutes.

Cinnamon
Kettle Corn

servings 4 **prep time** 15 minutes

A sprinkle of cinnamon gives sweet kettle corn an exotic air. Pack in a jumbo tin for a family-size treat or wrap single servings in cellophane bags tied with bows. For a touch of class, bag in cellophane and tuck inside a crystal wine bucket or a silver urn.

2   packages (3 ounces each) microwave popcorn, *Orville Redenbacher's*®
4   tablespoons butter
3   tablespoons water
¾ cup sugar
1½ teaspoons ground cinnamon, *McCormick*®

1. Prepare popcorn according to package directions. Pour popcorn into one or two large bowls (allow plenty of room in bowls to toss popcorn with hot sugar mixture).

2. In small saucepan over medium heat, melt butter. Add water and sugar. Bring to a boil and cook for 3 to 4 minutes. Stir in cinnamon.

3. Remove mixture from heat (be careful; mixture will be very hot). Pour half the mixture over popcorn. Carefully toss with wooden spoons. Add remaining sugar mixture and combine.

Party Planning

HELPFUL HINTS, TIPS, AND TRICKS

Entertaining is easy—all it takes is a little know-how and ingenuity. Creative gatherings are what this chapter is all about. The secret is to keep the basics simple and let details make the difference. The following items can be used again and again, and many can even decorate your home when they're not in use. Greenery, serving plates, and cake pedestals add interest to cabinet tops, and gold frames look perfect propped against walls and mantels. The rest can be tucked into a "party cabinet," where they're easy to reach when it's time to entertain.

MUST-HAVES: Simple white dinnerware; matching white serving plates; glass stemware—water glasses, wine goblets, and champagne flutes; flatware; serving spoons and forks; clear glass votive holders with white candles; stackable cake pedestals (in 8-, 10-, and 12-inch sizes).

DECORATIVE EXTRAS: Fabric remnants for tablecloths, ribbons, spray paint (in a selection of colors), ornate gold frames (16×20-inch oval, 24×30-inch rectangular), fabric ivy or greenery, 3-inch terra-cotta pots.

COLLECT OVER TIME: Gold and silver chargers; votive candles in a variety of colors (watch for sales and stock up); glass stemware—martini, margarita, and shot glasses; individual clear-glass cake pedestals.

NOTE: A tiny bit of creativity and imagination will go a long way toward creating a cost-conscious, picture-perfect Semi-Homemade® party.

SPECIAL THANKS TO: Petals 'n' Wax, Pier 1 Imports, Rosebud Cakes, and Hotel Bel-Air.

The Parties

Wonderful Wedding & Anniversary

Theme: This elegant celebration is a wonderland of white, with fresh touches of green and gold.

Centerpiece: Four simple white cakes march down the white tablecloth, each resting on a glass pedestal and topped with green grapes dusted with powdered sugar (for wedding cake variations, see pages 144–149). Petite vases of inexpensive white hydrangeas and gold hurricanes with white candles coordinate with mini compotes filled with gilded almonds and White Meringues (for recipe, see page 140).

Drink: For simple green apple martinis, mix equal parts vodka and sour apple schnapps with a splash of lime juice. Glasses of champagne stay chilled with frozen green grapes.

Music: Handel, *Classical Wedding*; Various Artists, *Great Wedding Songs*

Place Setting and Favor: Gold chargers elegantly showcase simple white china and clear glassware. Fabric ivy twirls gracefully up the stems of the martini glasses and around the bases of the fanned white napkins. The place card doubles as a favor—a large heart-shape bakery cookie, iced in pearly white with the guest's name in green, bagged in cellophane for a take-home treat.

Decorative Detail: An iron candelabra hangs from billows of white sheering draped to form the top and open sides of the dining pavilion. Ornate gold frames hung from satin ribbons give the illusion of walls. Both can be reused in the home after your incredible event.

Garden Party/Brunch

Theme: A mixed bouquet of colors makes a gorgeous picked-from-the-garden setting for a Mother's Day luncheon, warm-weather brunch, or stylish tea party.

Dessert Centerpiece: Serve dessert in high style by stacking three tiers of glass cake pedestals, each filled with deliciously drippy cupcakes iced with the word "Tea" in pretty pastels (for tea cakes recipe, see page 17). The cake topper is a sundae glass filled with multicolored hydrangeas, ringed with Mint Meringues (for recipe, see page 140).

Decorative Detail: A pale blue tablecloth makes a serene backdrop for mint green napkins and petite cake pedestals bearing Mint Meringues. A curl of green ribbon across each plate is the finishing touch.

Place Card: A personal handwritten note slipped into a matching envelope and propped against each guest's beverage glass makes company feel special.

Music: Mozart, *Great Piano Concertos*; London Symphony Orchestra, *Victoria's Secret Classics*

Beverage: Ice-blended limeade is garnished with sprigs of fresh mint and served in iridescent blue glasses.

Floral Favor: Large yellow and blue flowered teacups overflow with brightly hued hydrangeas, adding grace to the table and sending guests home with cheery memories of a delightful day. A take-home box of bonbons is another sweet treat for partygoers. (Simply glue silk purple posies on top of small white boxes and fill with store-bought chocolates.)

Birthday Bash

Theme: Bright bubblegum colors and a treasure trove of sweet-to-eats make a child's birthday party an imaginative retreat.

Favor Centerpiece: Whimsical take-home lollipop pots will draw admiring eyes—and eager hands—when filled with colorful candy and gum balls. So easy to make: Buy an herb garden planter from Pier 1 Imports®; spray-paint the stand white and the pots in a rainbow of colors. To set each pot "abloom," decorate with fun stickers, glue floral foam in the bottom, insert a large swirl lollipop, and shovel in candy.

Decorative Detail: The polka-dot tablecloth is a king-size flat sheet. Red folding chairs cost little to rent; add detail with miniature kites taped to the backs. Colorful inexpensive curly ribbons are cut from the roll and hung in the trees.

Music: Richard M. Sherman, *Mary Poppins: An Original Walt Disney Records Soundtrack*; The Archies, *Sugar, Sugar*

Dessert and Drink: Cotton Candy Bombs make a creative alternative to cake, and ingredients are store-bought to keep party prep simple. Arrange small scoops of strawberry and bubblegum ice cream on each plate, place a cloud of cotton candy on top, add a scoop of ice cream in the center, and insert a candle. The party punch is an old favorite—Hawaiian Punch® mixed with 7UP®.

Place Setting: Plastic tableware and paper napkins in mix-and-match colors make cleanup a breeze. Candy bracelet napkin rings and multicolored plastic souvenir Slinky® toys make fun favors.

Exotic Buffet

Theme: An exotic tapestry of earth tones and textures makes this Arabian Nights buffet a romantic choice for a sunset soiree, engagement party, or couples' night out.

Decorative Detail: Silky sari curtain panels cover the table. Sari wraps sway seductively from the trees, creating a tentlike intimacy, and cover pillows are scattered on the floor for casual seating, Middle Eastern style. Faux-jeweled bracelets serve as napkin rings. Presiding over the buffet is an inexpensive fiberglass statue of Quan Yin, the Chinese goddess of mercy and compassion, flanked by small iron Pier 1 Imports® candle screens, with tiny white candles beckoning guests to the table.

Firelight: A flickering flame ups the romance. The fire pit is a metal bucket with a ceramic planter full of kindling. A long wrought-iron votive stand holds soft pink candles.

Music: David Visan, *Buddha Bar;* London Symphony Orchestra, *Rimsky-Korsakov: Scheherazade/Capriccio Espagnol*

Food and Drink: Food is easy with Moroccan takeout—couscous, lamb skewers, roast chicken, and fruit—making a vivid counterpart to brick-colored pedestal bowls and platters. Red wine is served in pale pink glasses with gold etching—an exotic departure from traditional wine glasses. Phyllo Pie Bites are a sensually sweet nightcap of chocolate and cherry (for recipe, see page 26).

Macabre Music: Franz Liszt, *Fright Night: Music That Goes Bump in the Night*; Various Artists, *Halloween Hits*

Halloween Haunt

Theme: Shades of orange and black and gore galore create a frightfully festive setting for your Halloween haunting.

Beastly Buffet Centerpiece: Use a herb garden planter from Pier 1 Imports®, spray-paint it black, roll orange paper and insert one per pot; fill with caramel popcorn, doughnut eyeballs, and candy corn. Glue a black foam bat on top, drape with spider webbing, and surround with black votives.

Diabolical Detail: Lure guests into your chamber of horrors with hand-lettered invitations, each decorated with a glued-on spider. Drape torn fishnet stockings and icky-sticky spider webbing on windows and walls; add a ghostly glow with Chinese paper lanterns spray- painted orange and black. Dress the buffet in orange fabric, accenting with black paper napkins and orange terra-cotta pots filled with black plastic utensils.

Devilish Dessert and Drink Buffet: An orange-frosted ghost cake, caramel parfaits, and mini Oreos® served in Halloween baking cups make cool ghoul gruel. Downscale caramel apples to bite-size portions by dipping petite lady apples or crabapples in caramel and rolling in nuts, candy, and crushed cookies. Conjure up a plastic pumpkin filled with Witches' Brew—equal parts 7UP® and lemonade, tinted a ghastly green with food coloring. Add spooky smoke by placing dry ice at the bottom of the pumpkins and setting the punch bowl inside (use medium-size Pyrex® bowl). Use mini plastic pumpkins for cups (for all recipes, see pages 180—184).

Thoughtful Thanksgiving

Theme: Autumn colors and fruits of the harvest welcome family and friends for a grateful gathering.

Centerpiece: A black coffee press filled with coffee beans and tall cattails is a reminder of nature's bounty.

Decorative Detail: The table becomes the epitome of plenty when scattered with oranges, kumquats, mini squash, pumpkins, and pinecones. A gold frame hangs behind the buffet, which is draped with a faux silk remnant. A wooden chest holds wine bottles; a coffee press overflows with fiery-hued autumn leaves.

Dessert Buffet: Mini Pumpkin Spice Cakes (for recipe, see page 184), Sweet Potato Pie (for recipe, see page 186), and Pecan Caramel Cheesecake (for recipe, see page 21). Beautiful bonbons are simply small scoops of ice cream dunked in melted chocolate chips. (For melting instructions, see page 31.)

Music: Various Artists, *Thanksgiving: A Wyndham Hill Collection*; Vivaldi et al., *A Classic Thanksgiving: We Gather Together*

Sandra's niece Danielle makes a perfect Maple Syrup pecan pie. (for recipe, see page 186)

Place Setting: Use pinking-sheared brown corduroy fabric for a tablecloth, squash yellow tableware, and napkins tied with leather shoelaces. The place cards are tiny Hallmark® booklets titled for each family member (Mom, Dad, etc.).

Drink: To make heartwarming wassail, blend two cups of light rum, ½ cup of dark rum, five 25-ounce bottles of sparkling apple cider, and one carton of mango juice. Clothespin a silk leaf to each goblet stem.

Creative Christmas

Theme: Burgundy and gold give a rich twist to a traditional Christmas.

Decorative Detail: Burgundy feather trees sprayed with gold glitter adhesive sparkle behind a "chandelier" of faux crystal garlands draped from the ceiling. Gold hurricanes and burgundy votives cast a starry light over a simple gold tablecloth, overlaid with sequined gold sheering.

Dessert and Drink: A dazzling feast of fruitcake and cheesecake is both naughty and nice (for recipes, see pages 195 and 21). To create visions of sugarplums, scoop cheesecake into balls, insert a lollipop stick, and dip in white chocolate, nuts, and caramels. A merry Merlot is infused with purchased mulling spices and garnished with an ornament on a gold straw.

Music: Charlotte Church et al., *Our Favorite Things*

Place Setting: Clear glass plates are dressed up with inexpensive gold chargers and burgundy napkins wrapped in faux crystal garlands. Burgundy ribbon curls around the plates and petite cake pedestals holding store-bought ornament-ball cakes.

Floral Favor: To give guests sweet dreams, spray-paint stationery store boxes gold, glue a burgundy fabric rose on top of each, and mist with gold glitter adhesive; fill with gilded chocolate almonds.

Centerpiece: Four stacked squares of moss-covered Styrofoam® rest on pedestals of burgundy glass ornament balls. Burgundy organza wire ribbon cascades from the top, which is decorated with painted Styrofoam® berries, ice skater ornaments, and festive dragonflies.

Austen and his Aunt Sandy snuggle together, enjoying their family's holiday season gathering.

New Year/Black Tie

Theme: Whether it's a brand-new year or a black tie ball, shimmery silver and white help you celebrate in style.

Centerpiece: The best-dressed tables are wearing a head-turning centerpiece of fashionable white feathers. It's easy to make: Sprinkle a tall, clear vase with iridescent glitter, fill it two-thirds with rock salt, and insert 10 to 12 white plume feathers.

Decorative Detail: Special occasions call for glitz and glamour, so go all out. Make a festive backdrop by tacking silver lamé to the walls and attaching strands of silver disco ball beading (available at most party stores). Give plain white plates pizzazz with silver chargers and a veil of silver mesh netting draped over each place setting. Sprinkle the table with iridescent glitter, add iridescent white tea candles in clear votives, and scatter silver ball ornaments and silvered almonds around the table.

Music: Various Artists, *Pure Disco*; Various Artists, *Save the Last Dance* (Soundtrack); Billie Holiday, *Jazz 'Round Midnight*

Dessert and Drink: The toast of the party will be petite Tuxedo Cakes and clouds of White Meringues, served with champagne (for recipes, see pages 140 and 158). Top off the evening with Top Hat Shooters—just add two parts Kahlua® to shot glasses and very slowly pour in heavy cream.

Place Card: Use Super Glue® to attach rhinestones to white tented place cards; spell out guests' initials for extra glitz. Napkins are nattily dressed in black bow ties for men and rhinestone tiaras for women. (Tiaras are available at most accessory stores.)

Theme: Bold strokes of red and black bring happy harmony to this Asian-inspired table, perfect for an "Iron Chef," a Chinese New Year celebration, or Take-Out In.

Centerpiece: Put carry-in food center stage by covering a piece of plywood with a Chinese silk remnant and artfully arranging take-out containers and white bowls filled with rice, soup, and Asian entreés. Dangle a paper lantern from fishing line tacked to the ceiling.

Favor: Guests will feel fortunate indeed when they "take out" decorative containers filled with white-chocolate-dipped fortune cookies. To make, dip store-bought fortune cookies in melted white chocolate chips (for melting instructions, see page 31).

Music: Hans Zimmer, *Backdraft: Music from the Original Motion Picture Soundtrack*; Peter Gabriel, *Secret World (Live)*

Decorative Detail: Red napkins on white plates add a splash of color, echoed in the red votive holders and incense packets. Napkin ties do double duty as bandannas. To make, cut a white sheet into strips and use a red marker to draw a red dot—the Japanese flag symbol—on each; for Chinese New Year, draw symbols for prosperity, happiness, etc. The sake bottle cover mimics a traditional Chinese costume. A Chinese screen back wall keeps it cozy.

Dessert and Drink: Wonton Napoleons (for recipe, see page 22) and berry sake end the evening on a sweet note. For easy berry sake, combine one 16-ounce can wild berry juice concentrate, 1 cup crushed ice, 1/2 cup frozen raspberries (thawed), and a bottle of sake in a blender.

Index

Index (cont.)

Free

Lifestyle web magazine subscription

Just visit

www.semi-homemade.com

today to subscribe!

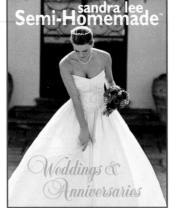

Each issue is filled with new, easy how-to projects, simple lifestyle tips, and an abundance of helpful hints. For busy people on a budget and on-the-go, the Semi-Homemade® Magazine is the perfect way to have it all.

tables & settings   fashion & beauty   home & garden   fabulous florals

perfect parties   entertaining & gatherings   gifts & giving

marvelous meals   music & movies   semi-homemaker's tips & tricks